# A Moth

The shockir... dangerous road to sanity

Alexander Sinclair

ATHOS
PRESS

ATHOS

First published by Athos Press 2019
This edition published by Athos Press 2020

Copyright © Alexander Sinclair 2019

ISBN 9781074053079

A CIP catalogue record for this book is available from the British Library.

ATHOS PRESS

*For my father, who was always there for me and proved to be my salvation.*

Disclaimer

This book is a work of non-fiction based on the life, experiences and recollections of the author. In some limited cases names of people, places, sequences or the details of events have been changed to protect the privacy of others.

# Contents

# Preface

It is now ten years since I published my first childhood autobiography, *Mummy Doesn't Love You*, a tale of triumph over tragedy. It would be a mistake, however, to think my childhood was without further trauma and adversity.

After writing *Mummy Doesn't Love You* I was mentally wrung-out by recalling the tragic events of my early years. In fact writing the book did me significant but temporary psychological harm, and it took me a decade to build the resolve to write this second book.

*Mummy Doesn't Love You* concluded with me going to live with my grandmother in November 1976 after my mother had tried to murder me, and ended on an optimistic note. However, the reality was that optimistic future did not happen for me until the following summer, by which time I had once again been taken to the brink of destruction, and faced demons that had the potential to destroy my mind. So terrible were the events that occurred during those months, it was generally believed by everyone that I was beyond redemption. The sole exception was my father, who moved heaven and earth to save me. The trouble was I had been rendered so incapacitated by the events of November 1976 that he not only had to persuade others to save me, but also press me to see I had a future that was worth living and not to give up on my life. However, by the time he decided to intervene my mother had once again used her malign influence and it was almost too late.

*A Mother's Revenge* is therefore a tale of the most potentially dangerous time of my life.

# Prologue

Hard hands grasped my shoulders and propelled me down the long dark corridor. Before me were six doors to six isolation cells. I cried out to the man not to throw me in, but he took no notice, just gave me a hard shake and kneed me in the small of my back as he forced me along. Another man ran ahead, opened one of the heavy pale-blue doors, and it gaped before me, heralding, I knew, the horrors to come: isolation by myself and a long pitch-dark night.

I refused to go in and tried to hold myself back, my bare feet slipping on the floor, just to receive another knee in the small of my back and a cuff across my head to make me move. I broke down in tears and let my legs collapse under me to flop upon the floor. The two men grasped my arms and dragged me into the room, where they dumped me on the floor. They retreated, slamming the door behind them.

I lifted my head, and beheld the small pale form of a child lying in the middle of the room; I knew Nikki was already dead; knew what was to come. I let out a scream... and was jerked back to reality.

I had had my flashback again, the horrific flashback and nightmare that has plagued me for forty-five years, ever since I was eleven-years-old.

I took stock of my situation. I felt the warmth of the sun on my back, stared at the sea, and knew I was safe. No one was going to hurt me ever again...

Love is a curious emotion, contemplated over millennia by philosophers, poets, and lovers. As I stood in the evening sun on my terrace, gazing at the Mediterranean, I too tried to evaluate this emotion. Love can take many forms, from the passion of lovers, to the unconditional love of a parent for a child, or indeed a child's love for a parent.

I sipped my glass of wine, my eyes fixed on the horizon, but my mind was far away.

Laughter from my villa drifted on the evening air, the sounds of guests arriving for an Easter party. Soon, I knew, I would be summoned, and my 'façade' – my bravado of being a normal person – would return, chameleon-like, and I would become the confident host once more. However, that 'person' isn't me, but I've become so used to using my façade in a lifetime of anxiety and tension I can no longer tell where one begins and the other ends, and that can be very worrying.

'Alex!' my wife Rosy called from the door. 'Our guests have arrived.'

'I'm coming now,' I replied.

I turned my gaze back upon the sun-flecked sea. The sun would set soon, I knew, and the sea would become ink-black beyond my terrace, ink-black beyond my cliff. With night comes sleep and then, I knew, I'd find myself reliving the past, and there would be no escape.

Ever since my father rescued me from a Greek mental asylum in 1974 I have feared the night. For me sleep brings nightmares and memories of my past. In a nightmare no one can help you, and I have dreamt my own death many times in forty-odd years.

Sometimes flashbacks will spring into my mind in glorious Technicolor, and I don't just mean visual memories. I can hear, see, feel and *smell* horrific things from long ago. Imagine being snuggled up in bed when suddenly a belt begins to beat your legs, or sat in a restaurant when your mind, unbidden, suddenly visualises a dead child and the smell of death invades your nostrils. The fear and anticipation that this can happen at any time is a terrible burden, and it can eventually wear you down.

All the psychiatrists I've asked over the years tell me these events are manifestations of Post Traumatic Stress Disorder, and I have PTSD very badly.

So why was I thinking of such things that warm April evening, the prospect of a party, good company and conversation ahead of me? The answer is I was contemplating writing another book about myself. I knew this book would be a battle for me.

Do I or don't I? I asked myself. And if I do, how far am I prepared to go?

What do you do if you know a terrible secret?

Well, the temptation is to tell someone, and it becomes stronger and more insistent with the passing years.

This story is, in part, a secret told to me by my father that involves me. I have known this secret for forty years, but I only 'rediscovered' it (i.e. was able to put names and dates to the faces and facts) when I recently found a file of reports and letters hidden in my late father's private papers.

*A Mother's Revenge* is the story of what happened when my young mind was overloaded by the psychiatric 'treatment' I had received from a German psychiatrist named Dr Edgar Schultz after my rescue from the asylum. As a thirteen-year-old I suffered a catastrophic mental collapse, triggered by my mother's attempt to murder me, which my British psychiatrist told my father was chronic and I would never recover. I was put into a mental hospital, and my father told I'd likely spend the rest of my life in an institution. However, my father *loved* me very deeply, and he never lost faith that I had the ability to recover. Determined to save me, my father fought all the psychiatrists to get me treated properly.

This is a story that ran to the final hurdle. I was within days of undergoing irreversible psychosurgery to control my condition; my father, a former Foreign Office diplomat, within days of making good his threat to use political secrets he possessed bring the reputation of the Foreign Office and the British government crashing down unless the treatment order was rescinded.

This, therefore, is the story of the most pivotal year in my life; the point in my life that could have gone either way. I could have become a child detained indefinitely under the Mental Health Act, a lifetime of impairment and incarceration ahead of me, or a youngster treated with drugs and care, and discharged cured with a future. However, the terrible truth is I brought this entire catastrophe down upon myself. Even worse, someone would die for me, and it would be *my fault.*

There is also, finally, a rather poignant element to this tale. I fell ill a child of thirteen. By the time I was cured and discharged my childhood was over, and I knew nothing would ever be the same again.

# CHAPTER 1

# Collapse

The flashing blue lights of the ambulance flickered in the night beyond the front door, and I knew I was failing fast. The way I kept pleading it wasn't my fault, the unpleasant expression on the policeman's face, the impatience of the paramedics, told me they all knew *it was*.

There was frantic activity in my grandmother's lounge as they worked to save her life, and as I stood in the hall I was sure everyone knew I had killed her. I heard my father talking to the paramedics in hushed hurried tones. I pulled at the policeman, but he firmly held my arm to keep me out of the lounge. I flopped to the floor and began to cry. I had done it again. Someone had died because of me.

It was the early hours of Wednesday, 30 November 1976, and I had been living with my grandmother for just two days when a disturbance by me at 1:00 a.m. proved more than her aged heart could take.

She simply said: 'Oh, my God!'

She clutched her hand to her chest and staggered away to the telephone to call for help.

My disturbance had been triggered by my mother's attempt to murder me with a massive overdose the week before. This caused me such psychological damage it let loose my horrific nightmare about the time when I had been an inmate of the terrible Attica asylum in Greece. So horrific was my nightmare that it rendered me an incoherent wreck crouched in the corner of my bedroom, beating my head against the wall as I tried to expunge the memories of my dream, of the things I had witnessed and experienced in the asylum.

I'd had a troubled childhood. To listen to my mother, I, aged thirteen in 1976 (but looking more like ten), was the worst child there had ever been, and she'd readily tell anyone who would listen – friends, relations, neighbours and doctors – that I was autistic, psychotic, and quite insane. However, this was not true. It was just that my mother had a talent for twisting the truth, had a warped perception of me, and a bizarre set of opinions firmly fixed in her mind. She could be very plausible.

My Greek mother was a psychopath. It gives me no pleasure to state this, but it is fact. She'd experienced a horrific childhood in Greece during the Second

World War, and the things she had witnessed had turned her mind. Outwardly a pleasant woman with a delightful laugh, she had a dark side once her front door was closed, a dark side in which there was nothing she would not say, nothing she would not do. I can well remember her favourite form of punishment for me for wetting the bed was to pour boiling water over my hands. My childhood was one of terror of my mother, a woman who was all smiles to her neighbours, yet a woman who was capable of inflicting excruciating pain on me just minutes later.

There is also no doubt that I had problems, largely motivated by fear of my mother, and this made me a highly-strung child prone to tantrums and easy tears. My mother's way to cope with me as a youngster of four, five and six was to give me *her* medication of Dexamphetamine and Valium in ever-increasing quantities. It was a recipe for disaster. The use of amphetamines in children can cause mental instability, even psychosis. Valium will impair learning ability, harming the interaction between short and long-term memory. In a cycle of decline, the more problematic I became the more drugs my mother forced into me.

By the time I was eight-years-old these drugs had taken their toll. My attention span was so diminished I couldn't learn simple lessons, and my school didn't want me because I was so prone to disturbances in class. I'd also cycle 'odd' behaviour. For example, given a toy car to play with, I'd hold it upside-down and spin a wheel, transfixed and mesmerised by the motion; the next day I'd do the same thing, and the next. I can see in retrospect this behaviour was a way of taking me out of time and space, a safe place where my mother could not reach me, but at the time all it did was present me as abnormal and disturbed.

At the age of eight, in 1971, my parents finally took me to be assessed at St Lawrence's Mental Hospital, where an unsympathetic psychiatrist diagnosed autism and retardation. I'd eventually prove this assessment incorrect, but it took me a decade. Like some terrible self-fulfilling prophecy my mother had proclaimed me mental, and her suspicions were confirmed by the psychiatrist. Mental defect was a terrible stigma to any Greek. My mother could not handle the situation, and she didn't want me anymore. With a ruthlessness worthy of the Borgias, my mother now began a campaign of psychological warfare to destroy me mentally, and then, she believed, she could get rid of me by committing me to an institution. In my mother's psychopathic world her family consisted of just her, my father and my sister, Vicky. I didn't feature in her plans at all.

My life became horrendous. With the assessment of autistic and retarded, my mother was at last free to use a range of powerful prescribed drugs – primarily the anti-psychotic tranquiliser Chlorpromazine – to control me. I was often sedated to the point of zombification.

Then, in 1973, came two life-changing events.

First, my second sister, Ingrid, was born in February. Just a few days later I suffered a psychotic collapse at my mother's hands, caused by her abuse and misuse of drugs, and was made very ill. I was sectioned and sent to St Lawrence's Mental Hospital. At last, my mother thought, she was rid of me. I remained at St Lawrence's for five months. However, I was treated and cured, and returned home in July 1973.

The second life-changing event occurred just a month after my discharge from St Lawrence's. My British diplomat father was appointed as Liaison Officer to the Bundesnachrichtendienst (the BND – West German Intelligence). It was an appointment that was to last one year. However, my mother not only refused to accompany my father to West Germany, she also refused to stay in Britain, claiming she could not cope with a mental ten-year-old, and a baby, on her own. Presented with an impossible situation, my father agreed my mother could take me and my two sisters to live in Athens for a year with her wealthy Aunt Elle. Sadly, my father had yet to realise how treacherous and deceitful my mother could be. Once in Greece, she demanded a divorce, then fulfilled her long-term objective to be rid of me by committing me to one of the worst mental asylums in Europe.

My committal to the Attica State Mental Institution was one of the defining events of my life, and I have never been the same since. The Attica was a horrific place of insane children and cruel uncaring staff, made all the more horrific for me by the fact I spoke no Greek and wasn't mad in any way. In the Attica a regime existed of profound neglect of the children on my ward, all kept naked in a bare locked room with teddy bears nailed to the walls, set against a ready willingness to use beatings, punishment and restraints to keep order. I actually saw children on my ward die, their emaciated bodies carried away on a stretcher once their torment was over.

It was in the Attica, however, that I made a lone friend, a boy of my age named Nikki, who had been put in the Attica for the saddest reason I know: he was just epileptic. Nikki and I became very close, despite the fact I spoke no Greek, Nikki no English, and we were in effect prisoners within our own languages.

Then, one day in June 1974, I caused a disturbance that resulted in Nikki and I being dragged away and thrown into an isolation cell. I was distraught at being placed in isolation, my memory of a similar event a few months, before when I'd tried to escape, foremost in my mind. On that occasion I'd been locked in isolation for two days, before being taken back to my ward where the two orderlies gave me a horrific beating with a belt. They then put a restraint on me and locked me, naked and bleeding, in an empty cell for a fortnight as punishment. By this means they broke my spirit.

On the day I was flung in isolation with Nikki I just stared at the door in anguish and terror. What would the orderlies do to me this time? I wondered. Then Nikki grasped my shoulder and turned me to face him. He suddenly laughed.

'Stop it!' I shouted. 'Don't you realise what's going to happen to me now!'

In a moment of madness Nikki and I, traumatised at being locked in isolation, began to fight, pushing and shoving each other in frustration and anger. Then we calmed down and hugged, but as I hugged him Nikki suddenly became still and staring. Then he collapsed on the floor in a catastrophic epileptic fit. He shook on an on, despite my efforts to hold him to stop him hurting himself. He flailed about, he beat the back of his head upon the floor, and his final sound was a choking noise when he swallowed his own tongue. Then he died.

I was distraught and traumatised to lose my only friend. I sat weeping and howling over him until the following day, when an orderly finally returned to find me in a terrible state clinging to Nikki's dead body.

I had been deeply traumatised by the loss of Nikki, and its Nikki's death that causes 90% of my nightmares. That horrific event pushed me over a mental precipice, causing me to suffer a profound breakdown that rendered me as insane as the other children on my ward.

When my father finally rescued me from the Attica in August 1974, what he got back was a mental and physical wreck that weighed just fifty pounds. 'Like a skeleton wrapped in golden skin,' in my father's words.

He took me back to West Germany where I received intense psychiatric treatment from a leading specialist called Dr Edgar Schultz. The trouble was Dr Schultz was an expert in treating adult trauma, and he had come at the recommendation of my father's colleagues in the BND. Schultz was the man who treated traumatised BND personnel – agents – suffering Post Traumatic Stress Disorder; men and women who had been rescued from behind the Iron Curtain. I too had been diagnosed as suffering PTSD as well as a psychotic illness, a PTSD related psychosis. Treat the PTSD, went the logic, cure the child. I was sent to live with Dr Schultz, and here he practiced all sorts of conventional and unconventional psychological treatments on me.

Schultz's 'treatments' began to have an effect after six weeks, and it became apparent I hadn't been mentally destroyed. However, what Schultz did to me had never been tried on a child before. Little did anyone realise, but he had planted the seeds of a catastrophe – a time-bomb – set to go off in the future.

Apparently cured, I returned to Britain with my father in November 1974, only to find my mother followed in June 1975 with my two sisters in tow. However, my mother did not return for love of my father. She returned because her money had run out in Greece, together with her welcome at Aunt Elle's house. She returned bringing her obsessions and her secret hate of me, as determined to get me 'put away' as she had been in Greece. As a child classified as mentally disordered and impaired my mother was determined to be rid of me.

In December 1975 my mother's campaign of psychological warfare against me began to succeed. Under relentless attack from her for months, the threats, the intimidation, the bullying – the violence – cracks began to appear in my mental well-being. My nightmares about Nikki became increasing virulent and I began to hear 'voices' talking to me. Dissociated from my surroundings, my confusion was often so acute I sometimes couldn't even remember my own home. Finally, it would appear, my mother had succeeded in pushing me over the brink into another psychotic collapse. By the first days of January 1976 I was so ill the only solution for me was admission to a mental hospital, organised by my social worker, Sally Martin.

I ended up sent to an excellent psychiatric hospital called Pen-y-Fal, near the market town of Abergavenny, deep in the Monmouthshire countryside. Here I remained, traumatised and ill for four months. However, my mother's plan misfired if she had thought she'd finally got rid of me. She failed to realise the differences between Greek and British mental care. In Greece the mentally ill are locked away and forgotten. In Britain I was treated, cured and returned. My mother's plan failed, but that did not necessarily mean she gave up, just yet, on her plans to be rid of me.

By the autumn my mother had become increasingly mentally unbalanced herself, as she became convinced my father was having an affair with the mother of one of my friends from school. Believing me the cause of upset in her home, her inability to keep her husband, in November 1976 she insanely decided to kill me, believing she could convince my father and the authorities that I had committed suicide with a drugs overdose. On Tuesday, 23 November 1976, my mother, in a terrible rage, beat me up and force-fed me three bottles of barbiturate, and I soon lay unconscious and dying on the sitting room floor.

It was now, with luck and the intervention of my social worker, Sally Martin, that my life was saved. I was rushed to the University Hospital of Wales, where I was treated and recovered.

My mother was now in deep trouble. She'd been caught red-handed, but the problem was I was the only witness to the attack. A decision regarding a possible prosecution of my mother was put on hold until I recovered from the trauma, and it could be determined I was in a fit mental state to testify against her.

On my discharge from hospital, after a five day stay to recover from the overdose, my father took me to my grandmother's house, where I was to live for the immediate future.

The siren was wailing as, with blue lights flashing, the ambulance took my grandmother away. Now, at the age of thirteen, I had my grandmother's death on my conscience, as well as Nikki's, and it was more than I could bear.

I sobbed whilst my father talked to the policeman. At some point a phone call had been made to Social Services, for two women now arrived to take me away.

In hindsight I can see I couldn't go home with my father; the authorities would never have allowed him to place me in danger near my mother again. However, I was just a child, distraught, and in the early stages of a mental collapse. In my confused state I thought I was being punished – banished – for killing my grandmother. I believed these women had come to take me away for good, and then I'd never see my father again.

I became frantic, sobbing and refusing to go with the women. My Dad produced my Valium, and the women and policeman held me and forced me to take the tablets. Everyone then kept me sat on the floor, talking in hushed tones over my head. I wasn't listening to them by this time. I knew they were going to take me away. How I sobbed that night, my voice hoarse and pleading.

Eventually the Valium took affect and I calmed down.

One of the women held my face gently in cool hands and peered into my eyes. She asked me if I was okay. I said it wasn't my fault. I pleaded I was sorry I'd killed my grandmother, and started to cry.

'Your Gran will be okay,' the woman insisted, but I knew she was lying. She'd say anything to get me to go with her. 'Now you must get up off the floor,' she continued. 'It's three o'clock in the morning, and we're going to take you to a nice place where you can go to bed.'

'Please, Dad,' I cried. 'I'm so sorry. I didn't mean to kill Nanny. I didn't mean it. Please don't make me go with them.'

'Come on, Alex,' said my father, forcing a smile I noticed didn't reach his eyes, 'Nanny will be okay. You have to go. I'll come to visit you tomorrow.'

Then, with the policeman on one side, one of the women on the other, they lifted me off the floor, and I allowed myself to be lead outside to a waiting car.

I had done it again. I'd killed someone I loved. I was truly cursed, and I began to sob uncontrollable as the car pulled away.

Underlying this traumatic event, my young mind was filled with the 'treatment' I had received in West Germany. A combination of Post-Traumatic Stress Disorder and Dr Schultz's treatment had created a mind in turmoil. If I wasn't having flashbacks, intrusive thoughts and suffering dissociation from my surroundings connected to PTSD, I was listening to Schultz's 'voice' giving me orders. His 'instructions' – his programming – on how to be normal: 'There is a wall between you and your memories; you must never look over it.' 'Do not talk about the past, because it will endanger you.' 'If someone tells you a joke, you must be friendly and laugh, even if you don't understand.'

Unfortunately, on the night of my grandmother's heart attack, my mind, in a state of trauma and confusion, began to make up new rules, and the 'voice' in my head giving me these new orders was that of Dr Schultz: 'They are going to take you away; trust no one.' 'They are coming for you. What can you use as a weapon?' 'Everyone hates you, and you're in danger.'

My mind, by now badly malfunctioning, began to lock me out, or even worse spurted into paradoxical panic. When I was locked-out I appeared catatonic, staring into space. When I was spurted in panic, it manifested itself as if I was completely deranged, beating my head against the walls to stop the 'voice' in my head, smashing the back of my hands against doorframes because the pain – the adrenalin rush – gave my mind clarity for a few moments. I also, sadly, began breaking glasses, light bulbs, cups and mirrors, anything to get a sharp object so I could stab myself, so I could slash my jugular, so I could kill myself.

This sounds insane, I know. Yet please recognise it for what it was. It was the insanity of a traumatised mentally ill child who could take no more. I lost no opportunity to hurt myself, lost no opportunity to cause an adrenaline-rush of acute pain that momentarily sliced through my mind's confusion – a mind that was plunging into catastrophic collapse.

It was in this state of mind that my father found me on the morning following my grandmother's heart attack. When I'd been taken away, I was taken to a children's home in the Cardiff suburb of Gabalfa, until Sally Martin could find somewhere more permanent for me to stay. The only other relatives I had in Britain were my Dad's brother, Uncle Tom, and his wife, Auntie Eileen.

However, before Sally could pursue this solution, I suffered my breakdown. The result was a child who was presenting as psychotic and looking for a way out. The only trouble was my way out was to kill myself, and then the nightmares, the terror, the guilt, the 'voices' – the orders – would all stop. So went my logic.

My father received a phone call from Sally on the morning following my 'murder' of my grandmother. Sally told my father she had received a disturbing telephone call from the children's home. The matron had told Sally she feared for my safety and didn't know what to do. My father immediately agreed to meet Sally at the home.

By the time he arrived, Sally was already waiting for him at the front door. She insisted they sit outside on a bench. They must talk *before* he saw me, she said.

'Is there something about Alex you haven't told me?' Sally asked.

My father forever remembered she kept twisting a lock of hair nervously, and her eyes had a haunted look. She was as white as a sheet.

'Like what?' my father asked, mindful of his secret orders to Dr Schultz to use his controversial treatments to eradicate timidity and trauma from my personality. 'You know what happened to Alex. If he's having flashbacks and panic attacks again he just needs calming down. He's had them before and you've seen them. He's become an emotional child, I know, but after what he went through in Greece I was told it's only to be expected.'

16

Sally was silent for a long moment.

'No, it's not that,' she said at last. 'I've been a social worker for ten years, but I've never seen anything like this before. You must see him for yourself, but you'd better prepare yourself. And please,' she added hastily, 'only stay with him a few minutes, then we've got to talk.'

As soon as my father entered the large nineteenth century house he knew something dreadful was occurring. He saw a dozen children gathered in the lounge, and a member of staff was keeping them there. Then he heard a horrific scream, high-pitched, feral, almost soprano, echo though the building.

'Dear God,' my father said, aghast. 'What's that?'

'That's Alex,' replied Sally.

My father took the stairs two at a time as he and Sally hurried to the first floor, then down a corridor, and the nearer he got, the worse the screams became.

There were members of staff standing in the corridor, and they looked bewildered and scared.

The home's matron, Mrs Wilson, stepped from the huddle of staff to speak to Sally.

Sally introduced my father.

'He's been like this since four this morning,' Mrs Wilson explained. 'Everyone's been taking turns to stay with him. No one can cope for more than half an hour. I've never seen anything like this in nearly thirty years. What on earth *happened* to this child?'

'It's a terrible and complicated story,' said my father.

Another scream shattered the silence.

'Please. If I can see Alex first,' my father insisted. 'I'll explain everything in a few minutes.'

Mrs Wilson nodded and stepped aside so Sally and my father could proceed down the corridor.

My father opened the door and entered the bedroom, just as another scream shattered the silence.

Inside he found the bedroom wrecked with overturned chairs, smashed glass from a picture frame, objects scattered everywhere, blood on the walls, and two women holding me facedown on the floor. One woman was sat on my legs and holding my wrists at my sides. The other knelt holding my head as she tried to stop me beating it on the carpet. My father saw I'd given myself a black eye, and there was blood coming from an ear. I screamed again, ear-splitting in its intensity.

My father fell to the floor.

'Alex... Alex...' he shouted as the stroked my head, trying to get through to me.

I wasn't listening to anyone anymore. I took a deep breath and screamed again, as I flung my head this way and that to break loose of the woman's grasp.

Sally grabbed a pillow and forced it under my head so that there was something between me and the floor.

'Please, Mr Sinclair,' Sally shouted over my screams. 'We've got to talk. We've got to take decisions.'

My father and Sally withdrew to the corridor to talk with Mrs Wilson, there to decide what to do.

As they talked a doctor arrived, and they stood aside as he hurried past. In a consensus they decided to wait until the doctor had given me a sedative to calm me down, and then Sally had action she wanted to take.

It was raining and the streets were slick and shiny. The windscreen wipers of the minibus flicked back and fore. Sally was sat up front alongside the driver, leaning over the seat-back as she talked to my father. My father was sat next to me on the backseat, and on my other side sat a nurse. I sat sedated between them. I was later told it was the same day as my collapse, by now afternoon.

My two overriding memories of that day was my head ached from the pain of the beating I'd given it on the walls and floor, and my sense of balance had gone as a result of the drugs they'd given me. A doctor had injected me with a powerful sedative so I could be transported to Pen-y-Fal Psychiatric Hospital near Abergavenny. I can also remember they took my shoes off to stop me kicking, and my father and the nurse spent the journey pinning my legs down. They both held my hands in my lap, my father stroking my head in a calming way during the journey. He also talked to me periodically, and said the same thing over and over again: 'It's okay, Alex... It's okay, Alex... You're going to be okay... You're going to be okay...'

It was as if he thought that saying this – like some magical chant – he could keep me calm and safe. I'm sorry to say he was dreadfully mistaken.

The minibus drove through the gates into the vast landscaped grounds of Pen-y-Fal, and despite the fact I gone completely bonkers I recognised the hospital I'd been sent to the previous winter. I struggled on the back seat, and screamed, dementedly, that they were all conspiring to lock me away.

'Please Dad,' I cried, frantic and pleading. 'I didn't mean to kill Nanny. I didn't mean it!'

'It's okay, Alex,' my father said calmly. 'It's okay, Alex.' Again the magical chant. 'I know you didn't kill Nanny. But you're very upset and ill. You've been here before. You will have to stay here again until you're well again. It's okay, Alex. It's okay, Alex.'

I began to scream, high-pitched and unending, as the minibus pulled up before one of the buildings.

I knew what this place was. They were going to lock me away forever now, and then my Dad would never come back for me. I became frantic.

The door of the minibus was opened, and just as my father was fumbling to pull my shoes on me, Dr Schultz's voice erupted in my head: 'You're in danger! Run! Run now!'

I shrugged off the nurse's grasp and leapt from the minibus, leapt out into the pouring rain, in just my socks, onto the wet tarmac. Two factors now thwarted my escape bid. The first was that, sedated, I had no sense of balance. The second was, in just my socks, I slipped in the wet, and fell sprawling in a puddle. The driver and my father grabbed me. I was helped to my feet, and there I stood between the two men feeling small, lonely, and very sorry for myself.

There is no way my Dad is ever going to forgive me now, I thought. He hates me.

I let my legs collapse under me and, bump, down I went on my bottom into the wet.

I began to sob distraughtly.

'I didn't mean to kill Nanny!' I cried, pleading I was sorry.

Everything happened quickly now. Two nurses ran out of the building and, just as Dr Schultz began to shout in my head that I was stupid and my Dad hated me, the four adults hustled me into the building. I was dragged, screaming at the top of my lungs, upstairs to the first floor, to the locked ward that was to become my home until, I believed, I was sorry for killing my grandmother, and my Dad forgave me.

If it had been possible at that moment, that November afternoon in 1976, I would have killed myself without a moment's hesitation.

# CHAPTER 2

# Sectioned

It was pouring with rain beyond my window. In the distance I could see the lush green Monmouthshire hills shrouded in mist. My fingers interlocked into the mesh screen fitted over my window, and there I stood, barefoot in my pyjamas, staring at the outside world. I can clearly recall thinking what a horrible colour pale green was. Pale green paint was ubiquitous at Pen-y-Fal, for my room had the same colour door, window frame and mesh screen covering my window, and I really hated it.

On the afternoon of my arrival at Pen-y-Fal, I'd been immediately taken upstairs to Ward 3, where I was placed in a secluded bedroom. There the psychiatrist, Dr Jones, gave me an injection to calm me down.

Despite the fact I was so frantic and upset, I remembered the kind nurse assisting the psychiatrist from my last stay at Pen-y-Fal. Her name was Judy Harris, a true angel. Judy was all smiles as she told my father I was in good hands, told him I was in the best place. My father looked lost and shaken. He just nodded, gave me a parting hug, then turned to leave with Sally. It was at this point I became distraught again, despite the sedative.

'It wasn't my fault,' I shrieked. 'I didn't mean to kill Nanny! I didn't mean it!'

My father fled and, as I leapt for the door in pursuit, Judy grabbed me. I watched as my father and Sally Martin hurried away down the corridor.

Made to sit on my bed, with Judy and Nurse Clark (a blonde woman in her twenties with bright blue eyes) sat on either side of me, I wept buckets that afternoon. Judy had liked me when I'd been a patient the previous winter. Now I was sure she knew what I had done to my grandmother. I thought she must hate me too. Indeed, I had the ranting voice of Dr Schultz in my head telling me everyone knew what I'd done, everyone hated me.

Regardless of Judy's attempts at conversation that afternoon I had refused to talk, refused to smile at her jokes, refused to cooperate. The only voice I had listened to was Dr Schultz, and he voiced my thoughts as they sprang into my mind. Schultz angrily called me abusive names for being weak and stupid. So there I sat, with a nurse on either side holding my hands. I just couldn't control my emotions that afternoon. One moment I was plotting my escape, the next I was weeping buckets. Judy tried to calm me. She assured me I'd be okay, assured me I was safe, but I was inconsolable.

Eventually, late that afternoon, a nurse entered my room with a mug of chicken soup. Judy took the mug and held it for me, telling me the soup would do me good. I held out my hand.

'Good boy, Alex,' said Judy. 'You know it'll do you good.'

She let go of my hand as I took the mug. The trouble was I wasn't listening to Judy. I had another, more insistent, voice giving me orders.

'Now!' shouted Dr Schultz. 'Do it now! It's your only chance!'

I slopped the soup on the floor, and whilst Judy and Nurse Clark's attention was taken for a second, I flung the mug as hard as I could at the window, shattering a pane of glass. I shrugged off Nurse Clark's grasp as I leapt from my bed, and in an instant I was across the room.

I picked up a shard of broken glass. Weapon in hand, I backed into the corner.

'Let me out!' I screamed. 'I didn't mean to kill my granny. Call my Dad, please, he'll tell you the truth. Let me out of this place!' I demanded to be let out of the ward, out of the hospital.

While Judy stood guarding the door, her hands held out in a placatory manner, Nurse Clark ran for help. I heard the ward alarm-bell ringing distantly.

'Let me out!' I screamed again.

'You know you can't leave, Alex,' Judy replied calmly. 'You've very ill, and your Dad brought you to us to make you well again.'

'Oh, please,' I pleaded. 'Just let me go. I'll be good, I promise.'

'We can't do that, Alex,' Judy said. 'Now, please, put down the glass.'

Just at that moment Mr Thomas, the male nurse, entered with Nurse Clark. His eyes took in the scene: the spilt soup, the broken window, me backed into the corner with a glass-knife in my hand.

'Alex,' he said firmly, 'put the glass down. Look at yourself. You've cut your hand.'

I looked down at the shard of glass in my hand, and saw for the first time the blood oozing between my fingers. I squeezed the shard and, crack, it snapped in my hand.

Just as I threw myself towards the broken window, Mr Thomas bounded over the bed and grabbed me about the waist. He firmly took the glass from my hand.

They're going to hurt me, my mind screamed as I flopped to the floor in floods of tears. But no, no one was going to hurt me.

Mr Thomas held me until Judy could take his place, and the way she held me bespoke compassion, not anger.

Dr Jones now appeared, and gave me another injection, heavily sedating me.

They then took me down the corridor and put me in 'time-out' (a ten-by-ten-foot white-tiled secure room). My clothes were taken off me, stripping me down to my pants, and I was dressed in a white knee-length cotton gown. The nurses left, locking the door behind them.

Time-out had no window, no furniture.

I curled myself up into a ball on the floor in the corner, my logic being if I made myself as small as possible perhaps Dr Schultz wouldn't be able to get into my mind. Every now and again Judy's face appeared at the little window set into the door to see what I was doing. I was doing nothing. I kept myself huddled on the floor in as small a ball as I could manage.

In the early evening Mr Thomas and Judy came into the time-out room. They gently helped me up off the floor and took me to my new room.

This second room was identical to the first, except they'd fitted a pale green steel security mesh over the window in case I tried to break that one too.

Ward 3 could accommodate twenty boys, aged twelve to sixteen, in three single rooms and three six-bed dormitories. Dr Jones had decided I was too disordered and disruptive to join the other boys at the moment. My entire world was going to be just my room until I showed improvement, and Dr Jones decided I was no longer a danger to myself.

My first day at Pen-y-Fal had been over a week ago, and since then I'd only been taken out of my room to use the toilet three times a day, and to have a wash morning and evening. It was a sad fact that I was so full of hate for myself that the nurses had to take it in turn to spend all day sat in my room watching me. I didn't talk to them. They didn't talk to me. Indeed, they even brought magazines with them for something to do, whilst they sat on a chair by the door guarding me as I sat on my bed. Their job was to make sure I didn't try to hurt myself again.

During that first week the nurses had to call for help on several occasions, for I'd become frantic and start beating my head against the wall. They'd inject me for that and put me in time-out, where I sat on the floor disorientated and dissociated, my mind numb from the powerful drugs they gave me. Also, because I kept hitting my head on the walls, even in time-out, 'head-banging' in their jargon, Dr Jones produced a padded-helmet which the nurses put on my head, strap bucked about my neck, to stop me hurting myself. I felt so humiliated in that pad-hat, and I hated Dr Jones for making me wear it.

I knew I was now at the mercy of Dr Jones. Until he decided I was well again I'd not be allowed out of Pen-y-Fal. The freedom of the outside world seemed so distant beyond my window that December day in 1976, as I stood watching the rain. I felt desolate. The world was now denied me, and I couldn't even go for a walk outside had I wanted to.

I heard the door open behind me.

I unlocked my fingers from the screen and turned my gaze from the rain outside to see who had come in. My heart sank. It was Dr Jones, and he wasn't smiling. In fact Dr Jones never smiled. Nurse Clark, sat by the door, exchanged a word with him, then he sent her out. I studied Dr Jones's expression. In my fragile mental state I studied every face carefully all the time, trying to work out what emotions people felt towards me. Was it hate? Was it contempt? Were they about to shout at me? In fact no one ever shouted at me at Pen-y-Fal, but it didn't make me any the less fearful it would happen.

It was a facet of my mental state, ever since infancy, that I could never quite work out a person's emotions from their expression. When I was eight-years-old, the psychiatrist at St Lawrence's Hospital declared I was autistic because I lacked this ability. Actually I was not autistic. It was just that since infancy my mother had mistreated me so much, smiled while she hit me, frowned when she was forced to be kind to me, that I had a limited understanding of emotions. I just couldn't *read* a person's face, but that didn't necessarily mean I did not try. I tried very hard, and that stressed me all the more. In fact I had developed the annoying habit of *asking* people what their emotions were. 'Are you okay?' 'Are you angry with me?' 'Are you sad?' I asked, as I constantly sought the approval of others.

There was, however, another element to my delusions, embedded since infancy. From a young age I believed my mother could read my mind, *knew* what I feared most, and would use my fears to terrify me. In my deluded state I developed the 'defence' of imagining I was eating a carrot. If I could occupy my mind with the feel, the taste, the crunch of a carrot, I believed my mother would not be able to read my mind. The trouble was, over many years, being repeatedly made ill, I began to fear anyone who looked me too closely in the eye was trying to read my mind, so I would automatically resort to my carrot defence. By December 1976 it was a serious difficulty, and it presented me as all the more unstable because, 'eating' my carrot, it would occupy my mind, my eyes would go blank, and I'd appear mentally isolated. Yet another autistic trait it was declared. I was now in freefall and no one could save me.

'Alex,' said Dr Jones, 'I've brought someone to see you. Now, if you're a good boy, you can have your visitor. If you get upset or angry, he'll have to go. Will you be a good boy?'

I nodded my head.

Dr Jones swung the door open, and my father walked in. He gave me a smile.

Was he happy to see me, I wondered, or was he trying to keep me calm?

'Oh, Dad,' I cried, and ran across the room to hug him. 'Oh, I'm sorry, I'm sorry,' I pleaded.

As I held my father I felt him go as stiff as a board beneath his sports jacket, taught and withdrawn.

'Oh, please,' I cried, 'don't be angry with me. Don't hate me. I didn't mean to kill Nanny. Please don't hate me. I didn't mean to do it.'

'Alex,' commanded Dr Jones, 'you're getting upset. Please sit down. Sit down now!'

I broke off from my father, glancing frantically back and fore, looking at Dr Jones and my father's faces, unsure what to do.

'Alex,' ordered my father. 'Do as Dr Jones says. Sit on your bed.'

Suddenly the relationship had changed. My father was taking Dr Jones's side. There was no one left who would defend me. Truly, I thought, my Dad must hate me for killing my grandmother. My father took a step backward towards the door.

So there I stood and trembled and shook. Tears erupted from my eyes and ran down my cheeks.

'You've got no one now,' Dr Schultz sang in my ear. 'You killed your granny, and no one will ever forgive you.'

I banged my head in its padded helmet hard against the wall, trying to disrupt Dr Schultz telling me his hate-filled poison, trying to get clarity of mind for a moment.

'ALEX!' my father commanded. 'Stop this now. SIT DOWN!'

I was sobbing uncontrollably by now. I flopped to the floor and beat my fists upon the tiles. Instantly Dr Jones and my father were on me. They manhandled me off the floor onto my bed.

I punched the pillow and beat my head against the mattress.

Mr Thomas appeared, and my father walked out. The next thing I knew Mr Thomas and Judy were taking me to time-out.

I was bundled into the room, Dr Jones gave me an injection, and I was gently, but firmly, sat on the floor in the corner. I curled up into a ball, as small as possible.

My Dad hates me, I thought. My Dad really hates me.

My time-out seemed to last an eternity on that occasion. Indeed, the senior nurse, Miss Johnson, even brought my meals in to me, and I was given a blanket.

The light in time-out was constant, a never wavering brilliant white glare in a brilliant white room. That time I stayed in time-out for three days. Three days of isolation; three days of medication; three days of no view and silence; three days of no stimulation. And always that bright white light. In the end, with no colours to look at, no shadows and no noise, I went to the other extreme of mental isolation. I seemed to deteriorate quickly now, for my brain began to create its own stimulations. Dr Schultz became an ethereal being locked in that room with me. Backed tight into a corner so I could take in the whole of the room without moving my head, I could not see Dr Schultz, but I could hear him so clearly. In the end I came to believe Dr Schultz's voice was coming *from* the bright white light, a light that hurt my eyes to look at.

One afternoon, returned to my room, Mr Thomas and Judy decided to give me a distraction from my anguish. They put a dressing-gown on me and took me to the Day Room, so I could sit and listen to a Christmas record being played whilst the boys on Ward 3 decorated a small tree in the corner.

As soon as I walked into the Day Room a big blond boy came bounding over. There was a broad smile upon his face, and I remembered him from my last stay at Pen-y-Fal. His name was Mark Stevens, and he was a sixteen-year-old schizophrenic who had been at Pen-y-Fal for three years. Mark was an intelligent boy, but he was also unstable and dangerous. During my last stay he'd become jealous of my friendship with a boy called Brian. Mark had attacked Brian with a pencil, and Brian lost an eye. Such was life on a psychiatric ward. A friend could become a dangerous foe in an instant. It did nothing to calm my state of mind, or give me a feeling of security.

'Oh, Alex,' Mark exclaimed excitedly, 'you've come back. I knew you would. We've all been wondering who was in Room Two. Oh, we'll have such fun.'

'That's enough, Mark,' said Mr Thomas firmly. 'Alex isn't very well at the moment. When he's better, you can talk and play with him then. Now please go back to decorate the tree with the other boys.'

Mark's smile turned into a scowl and he looked rebellious for a moment, as if he was about to argue. Then resignation came into his eyes, and he nodded and walked away.

I was heavily medicated the day the Christmas tree was being decorated, so I did sit relatively quietly – with Mr Thomas and Judy sat on either side of me – for twenty minutes. I listened to *Have Yourself a Merry Little Christmas* on the record player. Then it gave way to the soft voice of Bing Crosby singing *I'm Dreaming of a White Christmas.* Unfortunately I found the experience very upsetting, missing as I did Christmas at home with my Dad, and I began to weep. Some of the boys shot me uneasy glances, and two of the younger boys broke into tears as well. This was not the outcome Judy or Mr Thomas had anticipated, so rather than spoil the ambiance of a happy Christmas on the ward I was taken back to my room.

It was after this event that I seemed to become increasingly mentally isolated, and was now so heavily medicated all the time – zombified by the tranquilisers – that I became careless of my hygiene and began to have weeing

25

accidents. The nurses thus had to keep taking me to the showers, where they washed me.

I now screamed to the nurses on every occasion that I hadn't meant to kill, that it wasn't my fault. But they weren't listening to me anymore.

I was to later learn from my father that this state of affairs – in and out of time-out, medication, self-injury, and the sobbing – lasted nearly a fortnight. My mind in meltdown, I appeared to be completely insane.

Dr Jones explained to my father that he was sure there was much more going on than a psychotic breakdown, and he just didn't know what was best to do for me.

It was at this point, in mid–December, that my father, at a loss what to do, telephoned Dr Schultz in West Germany to tell him what had happened. He told Schultz that my recovery of 1974 had failed and I'd gone completely off the deep end. He told Schultz that Dr Jones believed that I'd gone psychotic, but that the psychiatrist was also sure there was much more going on in my mind than mere psychosis.

Dr Schultz was concerned to hear that my recovery had failed. He was one of the top men in Germany on Post Traumatic Stress Disorder, with an expertise in psychotic disorders, their cause and treatment. Dr Schultz told my father that I should be treated immediately to break my delusion that I'd killed my grandmother. He believed it unlikely my psychosis was due to a physical–chemical imbalance in my brain, such as contributes to schizophrenia, but more likely due to gross disorder, neurotic in nature. I must be treated before my mental illness caused catastrophic damage so pronounced it might become irreversible.

Between my father, Dr Jones and Dr Schultz an idea was conceived to break through my mental barriers and shock the delusions and psychosis out of me.

And so it was, on Thursday 23 December 1976, that I was in my room, sat upon my bed, Judy sat next to me reading a copy of *Woman's Own*, an arm about my shoulders in a show of affection, when my door suddenly opened and Dr Jones walked in with my father.

My father smiled at me, and said he had a surprise for me.

'Be careful,' warned the Schultz in my head. 'They're going to hurt you.'

Judy got up, and went to sit on the chair by the door.

My father turned and said something to someone who was out of sight, just around the corner. I heard a voice reply, and to my astonishment – and absolute horror – in walked Dr Schultz.

My mind was in turmoil.

It's me, my mind screamed. I've really gone mad! Dr Schultz has come to get me. His voice in my head wasn't enough. Jesus Christ, what am I going to do? I can actually *see* him!

'Hello, Alex,' said Dr Schultz. 'What are we going to do with you?'

'He's a fake!' shouted the Schultz in my head. 'I'm here with you. They're going to kill you now.'

How can he be both in my head, and in my room standing next to my Dad? And my Dad can see him too? I wondered, panicked and confused.

In anguish and absolute terror, I just sat, petrified, and trembled and shook.

'Not going to talk, Alex?' said Dr Schultz. 'Well, I've brought a visitor to see you.'

Dr Schultz went out of the door and spoke to someone. He returned to the room, a smile upon his lips below his white moustache, and I could see a woman behind him. Schultz stepped aside and there stood my grandmother, come back from the dead to get me.

I bit my lower lip in fear, and the blood ran free and salty in my mouth. I screamed. I screamed on and on in continuous shrieks of terror and anguish, and I couldn't stop myself.

My Dad, Dr Jones, Dr Schultz, Judy and my grandmother looked astonished and horrified as I threw myself off my bed and hid beneath it.

'It's dead people!' I shrieked at Judy. 'They're dead people and they've come to get me! Oh, please, God help me. Keep them away!'

This wasn't the reaction anyone had anticipated.

Of course, they weren't dead people. My father had told Dr Schultz I had suffered a mental breakdown, and convinced myself that I'd killed my grandmother when it wasn't true. My grandmother had just suffered a mild heart attack. I'd also been claiming that Dr Schultz was talking to me in my head. Schultz's prognosis was a type of delusional breakdown related to Post Traumatic Stress Disorder. He had seen similar cases often enough in his long career. He had advised my father the way to break these delusions was to confront me with the truth. Confront me with the fact that my grandmother was alive and well. Confront me with the fact that he – Schultz – could not be in my head if he was stood in the room with my father and grandmother.

Unfortunately, what no one – not Dr Jones, not Dr Schultz, not my father – took into account was the fact that I was now so mentally ill I wouldn't accept the truth before my own eyes. In my state of delusion I believed Dr Schultz had manifested himself in my room, my grandmother had come back from the dead to get me, and my father and Dr Jones were in cahoots with them.

To me the delusional world in my head was now more real than the world outside. This is an element of invasive psychosis. There is a misconception that schizophrenia sufferers' think they are two people. This is not true. Schizophrenia *really* means 'living in two worlds' i.e. the real world and the imaginary world. I was not, and never have been in any way, schizophrenic. However, I was now suffering a catastrophic psychotic collapse, which Dr Jones, at a loss to classify, decided to diagnose as schizoaffective disorder. The terrifying delusional – imaginary – world was now more real to me than reality. I was now in deep trouble, and Dr Schultz had inadvertently pushed me off the deep end. This was because I'd suffered so much trauma and horrific incidents in the Attica asylum when I was ten-years-old, the way I'd coped, the way I'd survived, had been to block out the real world. I had mentally turned inward upon myself to try to block the horrors I had experienced. It had been my immature coping strategy. The trouble now was I had resorted to this defence to block out reality on the night I thought I'd killed my grandmother. I was now psychotic and lost, and couldn't find my way back.

By now completely distraught and hysterical, shrieking they'd 'come to get me,' Dr Jones quickly ushered everyone out of my room. He then got Judy and Mr Thomas to get me out from under my bed so he could give me an injection of something powerful to put me to sleep for the rest of the day. In my current state of hysteria, the safest place for me was in bed and asleep. Dr Jones hoped that if I slept deeply enough for seventy-two hours, and then he gradually lessened the drug, I'd slowly come back in a more peaceful and less delusional frame of mind.

The white tiles of time-out ran regimented in a landscape of ice, separated by the endlessly connecting lines of grouting.

I sat on the floor in the corner, draped in a blanket, and followed the parallel lines of the tiles that ran about the room. 42, 43, 44, I counted, as the lines of grouting intersected each other, 45, 46, 47, Nurse Clark, 51, 52, 53. I lost my place. Damn. I started again, 1, 2, 3, and on I went with my counting. The repetitive counting chore seemed to keep my mind occupied and it kept Schultz away, at least for ten minutes here and ten minutes there.

I don't know how long I was in time-out after I flipped when Drs Jones and Schultz made the catastrophic mistake of confronting me with my 'dead' grandmother. Many years later my father told me Dr Jones kept me in a drug-induced coma for three days, which meant I was asleep over Christmas. Dr Jones then reduced the drugs until I gradually woke up. Unfortunately, if I'd been a delusional child before the mistake was made of confronting me with Dr Schultz and my grandmother, the child that awoke on 27 December came out of his sick-bed completely out of touch with reality.

I was now a child determined on self-destruction. I could stand no more and I wanted to die. I bit my wrists and hands until they bled. I kicked doors and walls barefoot until my toes bled and had to be bandaged. I clawed my face, causing wounds, and everyone was afraid I would damage my eyes. I beat my head on the wall so badly one day that I ruptured something in my right ear, and it bled profusely for three hours.

This was more than psychosis, Dr Jones told my father, and he didn't know what to do for me. He couldn't keep me sedated and asleep twenty-four hours a day, yet he couldn't allow me to tear myself to pieces either. He reiterated that he was sure there was more going on beyond a psychotic breakdown. My father realised the seeds of this catastrophe had been planted by my mother, which had then been inadvertently watered and nurtured by Dr Schultz, but *still* he kept Schultz's controversial 'treatment' to himself.

Dr Jones, checking my medical history for clues, now picked up on the fact I had been assessed as autistic when I was eight. This seemed significant to him, so he telephoned a Dr Edward Charles, who specialised in the care of Development Disorders such as autism, and described my condition. Many things now went drastically wrong, or so my father later believed. Dr Charles, unaware of my trauma in Greece, unaware of the controversial treatment I had received in West Germany, told Dr Jones that some autistics sometimes self-injure in a manic way when suffering a regressive breakdown. i.e. going into meltdown. He told Dr Jones that I must be prevented from injuring myself. Dr Jones, unaware that the autistic classification would one day prove to be wrong, became convinced Dr Charles had all the answers.

Dr Jones now began treating me as if I were a child suffering an autistic meltdown.

So there I sat in time-out, barefoot and white-gowned, the horrid padded helmet upon my head, leather mittens affixed over my hands to stop me clawing my face or biting my hands, completely dosed up on a cocktail of drugs. I was aware Nurse Clark was sat on a stool in time-out with me, but she was engrossed in her magazine and ignored me.

I started to hum a haunting tune my dead friend Nikki had taught me in the Attica. I didn't know the words, just the tune. My voice, high and piping, echoed in the tiled room.

Nurse Clark paused in reading her magazine to give me a searching look.

'Are you okay, Alex?' she asked. 'Do you need something?'

I didn't reply. I just carried on with my haunting tune. The nurses had tried every trick in the last couple of days to get me to talk to them, but to no avail. Ever since the visit of Dr Schultz and my grandmother, I'd not spoken. I just couldn't trust myself in whatever I said. Everything I said could be used as a weapon against me, so my solution was not to talk. I just kept crunching those mental carrots.

Nurse Clark stared at me for a moment. When she decided that I, sat on the floor in the corner, was not about to start beating my head on the wall again, turned her attention back to her magazine.

It was at this moment of relative calm that things, incredibly, took a turn for the worse for me.

The door opened and Dr Jones came in with a man I didn't know.

The stranger was thin and ginger-haired with wire-framed spectacles, and I took an instant dislike to him.

Dr Jones and the stranger came over to squat before me, and looked me in the eye. I avoided their gaze, and resorted to my carrot defence.

'Alex,' said Dr Jones. 'Will you talk to me? Will you tell us your name and how old you are?'

'Give the enemy no succour!' warned Dr Schultz. 'They're out to get you! Pretend you don't hear them!'

I kept up my piping tune, and I turned my head to stare blankly at the wall six inches from my face.

'See what I mean.' Dr Jones said to the stranger. 'No real reaction. He lives in a closed-in world of his own these days and we can't get him back. His self-injury is such a problem we're not equipped to handle such behaviour on a sustained basis.'

'Yes, I see,' said the stranger. He leant forward, rudely put his hand before my face, and clicked his fingers several times as if I were some pet to be teased.

I ignored him. I just leant my head forward to rest the pad-hat against the wall, and started my tune again.

'This is no good,' said the stranger, 'for him or for you. This is definitely an autistic breakdown. We are equipped with the staff experienced to handle this. I think it's going to be the best thing to transfer him to us.'

The conversation between the two men drifted on, but that is all I remember of that event, and even now, over forty years of clarity later, I can't bring back a forgotten memory. The reason I remember so much, even though I was so ill, is because of what happened next.

Dr Jones and the stranger stood up, and summoned someone from outside.

Then, to my alarm, a woman and a man walked briskly in, my clothes in their hands. The woman handed something to the ginger-haired stranger, who grabbed my arm and, before I could react, jabbed a needle into me and gave me an injection. The room began to swirl before me and everyone seemed twenty miles away, as gown, pad-hat and mittens were pulled off, and they dressed me in trousers and a jumper. A coat was produced, as were my slippers, and the next thing I knew these people had me on my feet and were hustling me down the corridor.

I soon found myself outside the building in the cold rain, and I was hustled, in a rather harsh manner, into the back of a minibus.

The man and woman climbed in after me, and pinned me down onto a seat.

I began to sob, despite the medication, and pulled at the woman, trying to break free.

'Stop it!' the woman ordered, grasping my wrists painfully and forcing my hands into my lap.

Moments later the minibus was leaving Pen-y-Fal, my destination God knows where.

# CHAPTER 3

# Calamity

For reasons connected to the privacy and dignity of others I shall not name the hospital to which I was transferred in the first days of January 1977, and the reason will soon become apparent. Suffice to say Dr Jones believed the ginger-haired psychiatrist, Dr Roberts, who was a specialist in Pervasive Development Disorders, namely autism. Mental assessments in Britain at that time were guided by the criteria of DSM II (*Diagnostic and Statistical Manual of Mental Disorders 2*). DSM II was the diagnostic scale used in the late 1960s and into 1970s, and autism was designated within it as a 'type' of childhood psychosis. Thus in 1971 my drug and abuse induced childhood psychosis was misdiagnosed at St Lawrence's Hospital as a form of autism. Since I had been mistakenly assessed autistic at the age of eight, now reiterated by Dr Roberts, this assessment determined what was to happen to me, and it would nearly cost me my future to live an independent life.

On the day Dr Roberts removed me from Pen-y-Fal, I was taken to a hospital in South Wales that specialised in the care of mentally handicapped adults and children with emphasis on Pervasive Development Disorders. For ethical reasons I shall henceforth refer to this establishment as Hospital X. Hospital X was not an institution of treatment and cure. All the patients had life-long mental handicaps and few, if any, were ever discharged. Hospital X was a large red-brick nineteenth century establishment, built in 1862, accommodating nearly 600 males and females, and it cared for a large number of children.

I was extremely delusional and confused in the first days of January 1977, and on my arrival at Hospital X Dr Roberts and the escorting male and female nurses took me through the large establishment to Ward B.

Despite the fact I was so mentally disordered, despite the fact I had Schultz ranting abuse in my head and been sedated, I can still, well over forty years later, remember how awful Ward B seemed to me, and recall with clarity the knot of fear I had deep in the pit of my stomach.

Bundled into the ward, I was handed over to two nurses who pulled my clothes off me and dressed me in pyjamas. I stared at the ward, and took in the reality of my new home. There was a continuous noise from the twenty boys on the ward, some of whom made cooing noises, some shouted, others squatted on the floor rocking. It was a ward of chaos, and regardless of how impaired I was by my own illness, I was terrified.

Once changed into pyjamas, a nurse propelled me to a bed in the corner of the dormitory, which I was told was mine from now on. I was then told I could go into the Day Room to play until teatime. Having seen the chaos of twenty disordered boys in the Day Room, I opted for the 'safety' of my bed in the corner.

I clambered onto my bed, which had a horrid disinfectant smell, and pummelled, squished and pushed the bedding until I had made a rampart about myself, my back against the wall. And there I stayed, weeping at the abusive taunts of Dr Schultz in my head.

I had only been in my bed for about an hour when a nurse came and made me get up and go into the Day Room for tea. Here, sat at a table with five other boys, I was given a meal of boiled fish and vegetables followed by jelly. Most of the boys just played with their meals, and I too just pushed it about on my plate, not having any appetite and still very sleepy from the sedatives I'd been given.

And so ended my last peaceful moments on Ward B.

I had a troubled first night, for with the gathering gloom of a winter evening, so my anxiety at the prospect of the night ahead – my nightmares to come – began to rise. I became agitated and began pacing the ward in a frantic manner, before collapsing to huddle on the floor because I could hear Dr Schultz talking to me again.

'Are you okay, Alex?' one of the nurses asked me.

See where your intransigence and determination not to talk has got you, I thought. I decided to break my silence.

'No,' I wailed. 'He's talking to me again. He hates me, and I'm frightened.'

'Okay, Alex,' said the nurse with a smile. 'I'll get you a tablet that will stop "him" upsetting you. Is that okay?'

I rested my forehead on the floor, and said: 'Please stop him hurting me.'

Well, I got a tablet that made me sleepy, and took the edge off the fear in my mind, the awful crawling sensation of terror in my stomach. The nurse then helped me up off the floor and took me to my bed, where I huddled up behind my squished blanket ramparts. The dormitory lights were put on, and the nurses began to wind down for the night by putting all the boys to bed. I just stayed in my bed because I was sedated and kept drifting off into fitful cat-naps only to jerk awake again every few minutes. At some point I must have fallen asleep properly, for when I awoke I found that my rampart had been dismantled, and the nurses had covered me snugly in my bedding. I watched the nurses make their last round of the dormitory, checking the boys, before they turned the lights off, and I, sedated, fell asleep.

When I next awoke, it was dark and the middle of the night. I could tell, bit by bit, that the sedative had worn off like the loosening of a mind-cloying miasma, and I was wide awake. I took stock of my situation. I was in a large dormitory of twenty beds, and it was dark except for the glow of light from the ward office casting shadows in the dormitory. I didn't know what kind of sedative I had been given, but whatever it was it left me bleary-eyed, dry-mouthed and I was desperate for the toilet. I also seemed, at the moment, to be having a respite from Schultz shouting commands in my head, and I can remember thinking, in my confused way, that perhaps I'd escaped Schultz and he had decided to leave me alone at last.

I got up from my bed and went barefoot to the ward office.

Two nurses were sat talking quietly, one busy knitting when she spotted me standing at the door.

'It's Alex, isn't it?' she said with a smile. 'Now what are you doing up?'

'Pl...please, Miss,' I stammered. 'I want the loo, and I'm th... thirsty.'

'Okay,' said the other nurse. 'Come with me to the toilet, and Nurse Wedlake will get you a glass of water. Is that okay?'

The young woman got up from her seat, took my hand and led me down the corridor to the toilets.

Well, I did get to use the toilet, and I got my glass of water, together with tablet Nurse Wedlake produced (another sedative), and that was definitely the last peaceful moment I had on Ward B, for my psychological respite did not last.

Later that night, at about 3:00 a.m., I suffered my nightmare about Nikki and jerked awake to the sound of Schultz shouting at me, and then my mother's voice joined in. I began sobbing and screaming out loud for them to go away and leave me alone. Placed as I was in a bed by the wall, I began pounding my head against the wall to stop the voices.

The two nurses were roused from their cosy office and rushed into the dormitory where I had awoken all the boys. Some sobbed in fear, others became very agitated and screamed in unison with me, and it took the two nurses about half an hour to restore some form of calm and establish I was the cause of all the upset.

Whilst one nurse went about calming the boys and getting them back into bed, Nurse Wedlake sat with me holding my hands as I sobbed and screamed, as I pleaded with her to stop Dr Schultz shouting at me. Again and again I banged my head painfully against the wall, and Nurse Wedlake was quite unable to stop me. What had been a smile when she had tried to be kind, became a scowl when she realised I was a source of trouble on her ward.

When the other nurse came over, Nurse Wedlake looked at her and said just one word: 'Seclusion.'

'Yes, the Seclusion Room, definitely.' came the reply.

The nurses dragged me from my bed, took me out of the dormitory into the corridor, and unceremoniously pushed me into a small bare room with a rubber mat floor. The door was slammed shut behind me. Then, to my absolute terror, the light was turned off, leaving my in pitch darkness.

As a child I feared the dark. As a child suffering psychosis and hearing voices, the dark terrified me because I could easily believe Dr Schultz, my mother, or even poor dead Nikki were hidden in the blackness. The light, the ability to see, gave me some form of grounding to know where I was, to know I was alone. In the pitch darkness I was terrified. I sobbed and screamed, pounding on the door with my hands, but no one came back. I was a mentally deranged child locked in a mental institution Seclusion Room, and no one cared.

To me 'seclusion' held many terrors. As a patient at St Lawrence's Hospital in 1973 it had been called the 'quiet room.' In the Greek asylum it had been an 'isolation cell.' In Pen-y-Fal they called it 'time-out.' I knew what this room was, whatever they called it.

If I had remained relatively calm and no trouble to manage, my life at Hospital X would probably have remained mundane, just one of long-term institutional care, and I'd not have had my future threatened by Dr Roberts. However, locked as I had been in seclusion on my first night at Hospital X, it just made my mental state worse.

By the following morning, when a nurse finally unlocked and opened the door of the Seclusion Room, she found me in a terrible state. Locked in seclusion with no supervision, no care, I'd resorted to banging my head on the walls all night to stop Dr Schultz shouting at me. The result was a bruised temple, a swollen battered cheekbone, a stunning black eye and a bruised split lip.

The nurse's mouth formed a perfect 'O' of surprise that I'd injured myself so badly. Such injuries would have to be recorded in my notes, and then some uncomfortable questions would be asked about how and why I'd been allowed to injure myself so badly overnight without any form of supervision.

The nurses immediately summoned Dr Roberts, who examined me. This done whilst I screamed frantically that everyone hated me, that there were voices in my head. He gave me an injection to calm me down. I was then put back to bed because I was so sedated. I slept all morning, and by the afternoon was recovered enough to pummel my bedding into a soft rampart about myself again, as I huddled against the wall. By now I had the voice of Dr Schultz shouting abuse at me again.

Far from remaining in a stable condition, I am sure in hindsight I was deteriorating. In the end, mentally exhausted, I slumped against the wall, and began to do the only thing that calmed me in those days: I began to hum Nikki's tune.

'Are you alright, Alex?' a nurse asked, when she came over to check on me.

I didn't reply. I had by now shut out the real world again, and in my traumatised and unhappy state I'd turned in upon myself. I just kept humming Nikki's haunting tune.

When my father came to visit me the following day he was upset by my traumatised and mentally isolated state, and very disturbed by my injuries. He was allowed to visit me on Ward B, and although the nurses had got me dressed, he was so concerned to find me huddled in a ball on the floor in the corner of the Day Room that he discretely took a photo of me with his miniature Minox camera (about half the size of a modern-day cell phone) he had in his pocket.

By now I was making no sense at all, rambling incoherently, in between sobs and screams, that the nurses hated me, that they were giving me poison tablets, and I wanted to go home. Clearly in the state I was in that was absolutely impossible.

I was a sectioned autistic child suffering a psychotic breakdown. There was no way I could be discharged from hospital, even if my father had wanted me out and in his care, which he did not. Instead, my father had a long talk with Dr Roberts, and the prognosis was not good. Dr Roberts announced I was very disturbed indeed, so disturbed in fact that he'd decided to transfer me to Ward C. Ward B was for medium autistics. Ward C was for the severe cases. Ward C was a comprehensive care unit for grossly disordered boys, extreme autistics and the worst psychotic cases. Dr Roberts said I was too disruptive to stay on Ward B. Ward C would be more able to care for me.

And so it was, after a mere 72 hours on Ward B, that I was transferred to Ward C, and found myself in a truly terrible place of grossly disordered boys, and overstretched impatient nurses.

If I had disliked Ward B, I absolutely hated Ward C. On Ward C the boys weren't dressed at all, but left in pyjamas or all-in-ones, like onesies but shabby with red hems and cartoon prints on the fabric. They screamed, they shouted, they threw themselves about, they wet and soiled.

Despite the very impairing nature of my mental state I can still remember by first impression of Ward C, and I have to say, regrettable, that I did not stand out as sane.

In fact I was so terrified by this environment that I suddenly and without warning wet myself, soaking my pyjama trousers and the slippers on my feet. Without more ado I was stripped naked in the Sloosh Room, where I was made to stand against a white tiled wall and washed down with hot water. They then put a diaper on me, plastic pants, and a shabby all-in-one that was so old the cartoon prints of Mickey Mouse had long ago been bleached into oblivion. I was then taken back to the Day Room, which had tables and chairs at on end, highchairs at the other, wherein sat the more disturbed boys. Abandoned in all this madness, I just flopped on the floor and curled up in a ball in my distress.

That day I sobbed and screamed that Dr Schultz was in my head and out to get me. I bit my hands and wrists until they bled, and I banged my head on the floor in an effort to destroy myself in self-imposed retaliation for killing Nikki and my grandmother. I was in a truly terrible and confused mental state, psychotic and presenting as completely insane.

On the following morning a nurse came into the Day Room with a wheelchair. I was put in it, a strap affixed about my waist to stop me getting up, and a small blanket placed over my lap. I was then wheeled out of the Day Room and down long corridors until we came to a door. The door was opened, and I was wheeled in to find myself in a visiting room.

Without a word, I was wheeled next to a chair, my back to the door, and the nurse left, leaving me quite alone.

After several minutes I heard the door open and close behind me, but because I was facing the wrong way I couldn't see who had come in.

Whoever it was stood in silence behind me, and then I felt a hand rest on my head for a moment.

'Dad?' I said.

Then the figure stepped in front of me and sat on the chair.

Her blonde hair glowed yellow, and the sun streaming in through the window reflected off her glasses giving her a strange eerie quality.

'Hello, Alex,' said my mother.

My hair literally stood on end to see the woman who just six weeks before had beaten me up and given me a massive overdose to kill me.

How she had managed to inveigle her way in to see me was beyond me, and despite my illness my mind still functioned enough by then to realise my father probably did not know. I also realised with rising panic that nothing good could come of this encounter. That she had an agenda, a purpose, I was in no doubt. I could feel tears welling up in my eyes.

'Hello, Mum,' I said as an automatic reaction, though every fibre of my being told me it was better to say nothing.

She was silent for a long moment, then smiled that sinister smile of hers. It wasn't a normal smile, more like a grimace, and it was when she smiled like that I knew she was capable of great evil.

'So,' she said, 'you've ended up in this place. I always knew you would one day.'

I failed to keep my tears in check and they ran down my cheeks.

However, an adrenaline rush of terror gave me clarity of mind for a moment, so I said: 'Why have you come?'

'Why, to see you, of course,' she said, and still that smile played on her lips. 'And to make sure they treat you properly.'

My alarm rose, for I knew by her words that she did not mean anything good. She had come to do me harm, and though I was out of her reach in this place, she had a malevolence and manipulative streak worthy of the Borgias.

'It's terrible here,' I mumbled.

'Oh, it's not nearly bad enough, yet. I've got a meeting with your doctor in a few minutes, and I'm going to tell him *all* about you.'

My adrenaline-fueled clarity evaporated and I broke down, sobbing distraughtly.

'You're finished,' she said. 'I'll see to that.'

She grabbed me by the neck of my all-in-one and pulled me toward her until my nose was an inch from hers.

'Don't think you're ever getting out of here to testify against me,' she snarled, her spittle landing on my face. 'I'll see to that.'

And with that she let go of me and smiled sweetly.

She got up and went to the door. I heard it open and her voice say: 'Can you come in please.'

'Is there a problem?' asked the nurse.

'The only problem here is my son,' said my mother. 'You do know why he was sent here?'

'He was transferred from another hospital. I don't know why.'

'He's a psychotic autistic,' said my mother, 'and he's dangerous.'

'Dangerous?' asked the nurse.

'Yes. Two months ago he threw scalding tea in his baby sister's face. She's now scarred for life. Then he tried to set fire to the house.'

'I see,' said the nurse grimly.

'Oh, that's just part of it,' added Mum. 'He breaks windows and attacks his sisters. He's extremely violent. When he can't injure people, he attacks himself.'

I could stand no more of these lies.

I screamed a soprano howl, and in my frustration and impotence at her deceit did the only thing free to me: I beat my head with my clenched fists.

'Now you can see what he's really like,' said my Mum. 'In my country we call people like him "weeds." They are just parasites, a burden who suck people dry of love and patience.'

'We have a word for them in this country too,' said the nurse. 'Don't worry. I'll see to it that you're not burdened by him again. He's here now, and here is where he'll stay.'

'Thank you,' said my mother. 'Take him away. I can't stand the sight of him a moment longer.'

Without more ado the nurse spun my wheelchair about and briskly wheeled me from the room.

'Goodbye, Alex,' called my mother sweetly and mellifluously, but I was not deceived. She had a streak of evil a mile wide, and she had just ruined me.

I screamed and hollered as I was wheeled away down the corridor, and continued to beat my head with my fists, only to receive a hard slap across the head.

'Bad boy,' said the nurse. 'Be quiet.'

I was later to learn this nurse was named Banks. She had been effectively turned against me and now saw me as deranged and dangerous, and soon she would become my most obdurate enemy.

Once back in the Day Room, as I continued to scream and beat at my head, two nurses came over to me sat in the wheelchair.

'What's happened?' asked one of the nurses.

'He's having a tantrum,' replied Nurse Banks. 'I'll tell you what his mother told me about him in a moment, but first let's get him in a highchair before he injures himself or someone else, and I think we'd better give him a sedative.'

With me kicking and screaming, the three nurses got me out of the wheelchair and secured me in a highchair with the pommel and waist-strap affixed to stop me getting up. My sleeve was rolled up and one of the nurses injected me. The nurses then tied my wrists with a bandage and secured them to the pommel. All three nurses then held me still until I calmed down, one with an arm held tightly about my neck to keep my head still. My mind drifted off into a world of non-reality, and all the while ringing in my ears were my mother's words: 'Goodbye, Alex.'

Having been completely undone by my mother, and in no small part made distraught that she was now making it her mission to ensure I stayed detained in this place, any ethereal sanity I still possessed abandoned me. I spent all my days secured in that highchair, sobbing and screaming. I lost control of my bowels and was unclean, and they drugged me up to the eyeballs. The only respite from the highchair was a twice daily trip to the Sloosh Room to be washed and changed.

After what seemed like an eternity, but was probably only a few days, I awoke from my drugged doziness one day to see Dr Roberts and Nurse Banks stood before me in conversation. I don't know, or remember, what was said, but Dr Roberts reached forward, lifted one of my eyelids with his thumb, and had a good look into my eye. All I recall he said was: 'Sodium Amytal.' Then he left.

Thereafter my days passed in a drug-induced haze.

I had reached rock bottom.

On my arrival at Hospital X I had looked upon my fellow inmates with contempt and pity. Now I was probably one of the worst cases there.

Looking back with the hindsight of forty-odd years of sanity I wonder why I did not feel terror at the time that this was probably going to be my life from now on, but to be frank by then I was so far gone my mind was no longer capable to think of such things.

It was in this state that one afternoon Nurse Banks put me in a wheelchair, a strap about my waist to keep me seated, and took me off the ward. I had no idea where she was taking me and I did not dare ask, because by now Nurse Banks hated me, and I greatly feared her.

The night after my mother's visit I suffered my terrifying nightmare about the death of Nikki, and disturbed the ward in the middle of the night. Nurse Banks had been on duty, but rather than show any compassion towards me she had pulled me from my bed and dragged me to the Seclusion Room. There she produced a tight-fitting bag like a pillowcase made of canvas, which she pulled over my torso, my head to pop out of a hole in the closed end. She then secured the pillowcase over my torso and arms by pulling a cloth strip between my legs and securing it at the small of my back. In this restraint I could not use my hands or arms. Nurse Banks then locked me in the pitch-dark of the Seclusion Room. I had huddled in a ball on the floor and sobbed the entire night away. Nurse Banks only let me out of the pillowcase and put me back to bed at the end of her shift. As a result I was terrified of Nurse Banks. She had been effectively turned against me by my mother's lies, and now saw me as deranged and dangerous.

On the day Nurse Banks took me off the ward I had no idea where she was taking me, until, after many corridors, she took me into the Visiting Room, and there stood my father.

'Daddy,' I cried, reaching for him.

My father took my hands and smiled.

'It's okay, Alex,' he said. "It's okay, now. These nice people will make you well again."

'No, no. They hate me,' I sobbed in anguish, my words slurring. 'Please take me home.'

'That's not possible, Alex,' my father said firmly. "You have to stay here until you're well again.'

'No!' I screamed, getting very upset.

I began to sob distraughtly, frantically trying to get up from the wheelchair. Nurse Banks pushed me back to sit down.

'This is no good, Mr Sinclair,' she said to my father. "Alex is getting very distressed and agitated. I must take him back to the ward."

'Yes,' said my father with a look of resignation on his face. 'I think you'd better.'

'No!' I shrieked hysterically, but by now Nurse Banks had spun my wheelchair about and taken me out of the room, away from my Dad, heading back to the ward.

I sobbed and screamed all the way back, making a terrible din. My reward for misbehaving, a soon as I was out of my father's sight, was a hard slap across the head and, ultimately, I ended up placed in seclusion for the rest of the afternoon.

Seclusion was awful. The Seclusion Room in Ward C was reminiscent of time-out at Pen-y-Fal, about ten-feet-by-ten square, with no window except for a small pane of glass set high up in the door so the nurses could peek in to see what I was doing. The rather horrible difference here was the room had rubber mats affixed to the walls and floor.

In seclusion I usually did nothing except curl up in a ball in the corner, making myself as small as possible, hoping that if I made myself small enough Dr Schultz would leave me alone. Sadly it never worked, and I was periodically subjected to Schultz's commands of 'Keep still!' 'Don't move!' 'Stop thinking!' I could even feel him grabbing my hands and arms (i.e. I was having tactile hallucinations). Worse, he often had the ability to voice my thoughts as they entered my mind, something that is today called 'commentary.' As a mere child I didn't understand it was an illness of my mind. Lacking insight, I genuinely believed Dr Schultz was invisible, or his voice was coming out of the walls. The consequence was I became very confused indeed as I screamed at him to leave me alone, or flung myself about the room beating my head on the rubber walls.

Deranged of mind, my time on Ward C seemed endless, during which things became very bad for me, and this was in no small part due to Nurse Banks.

As a mentally disordered child I cannot say in any honesty that I was easy to manage, and this was especially the case at night.

At the end of January, I began to suffer increasingly virulent and horrific nightmares about Nikki, and I always awoke screaming in terror. Nurse Banks was totally unsympathetic to my plight. If I screamed in terror this woke the other boys, so Nurse Banks would yank me from my bed and bundle me into the corridor where she locked me in seclusion for the rest of the night. Unfortunately, Nurse Banks really took against me, and was harsh and completely unsympathetic. She soon began to lock me in seclusion every time she was on duty.

I suppose it was my own fault, because I soon made the situation worse. Locked in seclusion in the pitch dark one night, I started screaming, imagining all sorts of horrors hidden in the darkness with me. It was now that Nurse Banks showed her true sadistic streak, and any sanity I still possessed, as precarious as it was, was placed in peril.

Obviously my screams would carry through the Children's Unit to the other wards and invite comment, so one night Nurse Banks flew into the Seclusion Room to shut me up and gave me a sharp slap across the face. She then dragged me by my hair to the Shower Room, where she pulled my all-in-one and diaper off me and gave me an ice-cold shower. She then beat me with a wet towel. Every lash of the towel stung like mad and left me in agony. She then took my clothing away and locked me in the Shower Room. Left naked, cold and shivering, I sobbed the entire night away, huddled on the floor in the corner.

This now became a common event virtually every night, for instead of seclusion Nurse Banks would take me from my bed and give me a cold shower as punishment for waking the ward. Every time I made a noise, shouted or screamed, Nurse Banks or another woman would burst into the Shower Room and beat me with a wet towel, before giving me another ice-cold shower. These events could occur as often as two or three times a night.

Naturally, my already fragile mental state began to suffer, and this made me seem all the more mentally unstable. In the daytime – and probably suffering sleep deprivation as well by now – I became all the more problematic to manage. I now spent my days sedated and secured in the highchair in the corner of the Day Room. I refused to eat and I refused to cooperate in any way. Instead, I used any opportunity to injure myself by beating my head with my fists, on one occasion so badly I nearly broke my nose and gave myself two black eyes. After that event they bound my hands to the pommel with a bandage all the time. Yet through all this, all this insanity, all this screaming, all my hallucinations of Dr Schultz ordering me about, I now lived in terror of every night, not so much now because of fear of my nightmares, but because I feared the ice-cold showers, beatings and being left locked in the Shower Room.

As a child classified as autistic, psychotic and deranged, I can see in hindsight why no one believed me when, in my more lucid moments, I pleaded with anyone, from nurses to cleaners to let me go home. I screamed to my father when he came to visit me that the nurses were horrible to me, that they hurt me and I didn't like being locked in the Shower Room at night. Yet even as I rambled these things to my father I could see by the expression on his face that he didn't believe the rantings of his psychotic son. He would kneel before me holding my hands, gazing at the latest bruises on my face, my black eyes. Then he'd look up at the escorting nurse who'd shake her head indicating that I was talking nonsense again. A look of resignation would come over his face, and he'd smile sadly and say: 'It's okay, Alex. You'll be better one day, and then you can come home.'

'No!' I'd shriek. 'Everyone hates me. They hurt me, Dad. They hurt me!'

'It's okay, Alex,' my father would say calmly. 'I'll make sure you're not hurt again. Now just stay calm. Can you do that for me?'

At this I'd scream in frustration because no one believed me. My Dad would end his visit, and I was taken back to the ward; there to fear the night ahead.

I suppose the worst aspect was, as ill as I was, no one believed a word I said. After all, how could my father differentiate between my claims that Dr Schultz was talking to me, that I'd felt my mother grabbing my arms, *or* that the nurses hurt me with painful hidings and gave me ice-cold showers in the middle of the night.

In the end I finally understood no one accepted a word I said, and that was almost as bad as my dreaded fear of the 'voices.' I was a mentally ill child who was allegedly insane and everyone thought I was rambling deranged nonsense. No one believed a word I said anymore, and that, in itself, was terrifying too.

# CHAPTER 4

# Peril

B y the first days of February I was no longer coherent in any form. Drugged into oblivion, I was totally incontinent and had lost the ability to think. They were even feeding me half the time. I have effectively become... a cabbage. It is therefore not possible to recount my experiences of February 1978, with the exception of a few memories. There is nothing to tell anyway, for I suspect my days and nights were the same as January, most of which I unfortunately do remember. However, events were now to take place involving my father, which he recounted to me five years hence, so although this chapter is told from my point of view it is really the story of how my father saved me.

Despite the fact I was extremely mentally ill and disordered, and as a consequence no one took anything I said seriously anymore – from my declarations that Dr Schultz was in my head, to my claims I'd killed Nikki and my grandmother – something I said to my father in mid-February caused him deep concern. It came at a time when he finally understood I was in peril. It would shatter his faith in the medical profession, as he, at long last, realised he had a battle on his hands to save me; not my life, but my very personality.

On Monday, 14 February, my father came to visit me at the hospital, and I was taken to the Visiting Room in all-in-one by wheelchair. On this occasion I was taken to see my father by a young nurse, who I will call 'Miss T.' Once again, as usual, my Dad knelt before me, took my hands in his, and stared deep into my eyes.

'Hello, Alex,' he said gently. 'How are you, son? I see you've given yourself another black eye. You must try not to do that you know.'

'Oh, please, Dad,' I said, starting to cry, my speech disorganised and rambling. 'They're horrible to me. They take my clothes away and lock me in the dark. I hate it here. I hate it. They give me cold showers and lock me in the Shower Room.'

'Now come on, Alex,' my father replied. 'That's not true. So long as you keep telling lies like this it's going to take you longer to get better.'

'It's not a lie!" I screamed.

My father gave me one of his resigned expressions, and raised his eyes to the young nurse, but something on her face made his heart miss a beat, and his mouth took on a firm line of determination as he stood up.

'Tell me,' my father said to the nurse, 'is anything my son has said true?'

The nurse let go of the wheelchair and dashed to the door to peek out, making sure there was no one about. She closed it and came back.

'Yes,' she said, 'some of the things are true. Things happen here, you know. But for God's sake please don't tell anyone what I've told you. I'll lose my job.'

The young nurse then went on to tell my father that a regime of mistreatment and abuse existed in the hospital. It was not widespread, but it did happen, and the patients – especially the children – had no one to defend them.

My father pointedly asked Miss T if I was being abused, to which Miss T shrugged and said it was possible. She knew Nurse Banks seemed to have taken against me and, yes, one night she'd been on duty she'd seen me given cold showers for being disruptive.

'Look,' said the nurse finally, 'I can't talk here. We might be overheard, and I can't talk in front of Alex in case he repeats something I say to you. Meet me at the *Red Lion* pub on the Cowbridge Road at six o'clock, and I'll talk to you then.'

My father agreed, and that was the end of the visit, for Miss T took me back to the ward.

However, that was not to be the end of my father's traumatic day, for within the hour he was sat in Dr Roberts' office, and what the psychiatrist told him left him speechless and in shock.

Dr Roberts told my father that I was definitely a chronically psychotic autistic, and as such unlikely to ever recover. He ventured to suggest that as a grossly autistic child it would explain why my behavioural problems – isolated and lonely behaviour, poor cognitive skills, bizarre behavioural traits, and self-injury – were becoming more pronounced with age, which had now become exacerbated by delusional psychosis. As a result my behaviour was becoming increasingly aggressive and violent, in terms of self-injury, and this would only get worse, and more difficult to manage, as I got older.

Dr Roberts stated that because autism was a life-long condition, and my psychosis was chronic, I would probably never be released. Therefore my long-term hospital care must now be considered, with particular emphasis to my aggressive self-injury. At the moment I was a small thirteen-year-old, akin to a ten-year-old in size, and the nurses could just about manage me, even if that meant putting me in seclusion rather more often than was desirable until I calmed down. However, taking no action was not an option, for as I grew into a juvenile and then a young adult, my aggressive behaviour and self-injury would become very difficult to manage; difficult for the nurses, and difficult – unpleasant – for me.

My father considered these points, and conceded they were valid if, and only if, I failed to recover.

At that remark Dr Roberts slammed his pencil down on the desk.

'Look, Mr Sinclair,' he said, 'in my opinion Alex won't ever recover.'

'Well, doctor,' my father replied, 'we'll have to agree to differ. Alex has recovered in the past, and I believe he'll recover in the future.'

'No, Mr Sinclair,' Dr Roberts retorted, 'we cannot agree to differ. Alex is too agitated and violent for his condition to be managed by drugs alone. I have scheduled him for a leucotomy at Whitchurch Hospital on Tuesday, 1 March.'

My father was deeply shocked and devastated at this news. A leucotomy is an operation on the brain to cut a bundle of nerves connecting the two frontal lobes. It is conducted by inserting an instrument into the brain through an eye socket. It was a common operation in Britain in the 1960s and 1970s. Indeed Whitchurch Hospital in Cardiff is the only place in Britain that still conducts leucotomy operations to this day. In successful cases aggressive patients become calm and malleable, but their personalities are often altered. In unsuccessful cases, such as happened to President John F. Kennedy's sister, the patient can be reduced to an incoherent cabbage, and destined for a life in care.

'I object!' my father declared. 'I object most strongly, and I forbid you to operate on my son!'

'I'm sorry, Mr Sinclair,' Dr Roberts retorted, 'but I don't need your permission. Alex is a sectioned patient, and I am authorised, as his practitioner, to take all his care and welfare decisions.'

There then followed a heated argument, during which my father lost his temper and stormed out.

Many years later my father told me his meeting with Dr Roberts that day left him cold and petrified for me. The idea that the doctor could order my brain cut – my personality altered – without his permission, nearly drove him to despair. If that was not bad enough, he had just learnt that my claims of abuse, of being given cold showers, locked up and hurt might just turn out to be true. My father contemplated the fact I was now detained, legally, in a place he did not want me in, and I might have to stay there forever, *unless* he could find a way to spring me out.

That same day, at 6:00 p.m., he went to the *Red Lion* pub to meet Miss T, and what she told him confirmed his worst fears.

Miss T told my father, most confidentially, that she'd seen the staff hit patients, and there was a high degree of physical restraint used rather more often than necessary. When my father asked Miss T to make a formal statement, the young woman said she had only been a nurse for a year, and Hospital X was her first position. She refused, saying she feared bullying and intimidation by the other members of staff and she might even lose her job. Instead, Miss T agreed to keep her eyes open, and my father gave her his miniature Minox camera to take secret pictures of the conditions in Hospital X, especially any she could take of me. Miss T agreed to do this for my father, her parting words: 'I became a psychiatric nurse to care for patients, not to bully them or stand by and watch them being mistreated.'

'Please,' my father urged, 'act quickly. Take as many pictures as you can.' He handed her his card, adding: 'Please come to my house on Friday at six o'clock. I only have fourteen days to save my son from having to undergo a leucotomy. Every day is precious.'

Luckily for me, my father was a well-connected former diplomat of the Foreign Office. In the 1950s and '60s he'd been an officer of the Political Intelligence Division, which was an organ of the intelligence service of the Foreign Office. My father was now a senior lecturer in politics and economics at Cardiff University, and he was currently an intermediary for the Israeli government in their secret peace talks with Egypt. All this meant my father knew many important people in his long career.

My father realised the normal routes of appeal to Dr Roberts would be useless. Dr Roberts was a prominent psychiatrist, a man determined to treat me in a way he saw fit. His influence would not help if he just went over Dr Roberts' head. *His* contacts meant he needed to go to the very top.

My father was always full of many sayings and witty quotes, but the one that sprang to mind that day was: 'Speak softly, but carry a big stick.'

From what he now knew about the regime at Hospital X, and the significant fact he wanted the leucotomy cancelled, he would need to go to the very top of the National Health Service *and* use his most explosive tools to get me out. In short, my father decided to go directly to the Secretary of State for Health, David Ennals MP, and the Cabinet Secretary, Sir John Hunt.

On the evening of Friday 18 February, Miss T arrived at my father's house, and to her shock found my father's lawyer present to take down her statement. At first Miss T was upset that my father was pressurising her into giving a formal statement and she was reluctant to talk, until my father and his lawyer gave her an assurance that her name would be kept confidential. In the end Miss T understood it was important for her evidence to be given on a formal basis.

Miss T was given a cup of coffee while the lawyer prepared his papers, and over the course of the next four hours her coffee was left cold and forgotten. Miss T talked late into the night, and the tale she told made my father's blood run cold to think of me being held as a detained patient in Hospital X. My Dad knew my ordeal in the Attica had been appalling, but the conditions there had emanated from ignorance and backward practice. What my father heard was taking place in Hospital X emanated from a lack of compassion, and in some cases actual cruelty.

Miss T told a tale of an institution in which a lack of care and complacency at abuses predominated. It was not so much that certain staff member were cruel (which they were), but rather more the case that all the patients had lifelong handicaps, and the hospital's senior staff let the lower ranks take shortcuts to manage the very disordered patients, and this led to abuses. As a result a regime of fear existed. The nursing staff bullied the patients, and this sometimes extended to physical abuse such as hitting them. The Seclusion Room was more often used as a first resort instead of a last resort, and the staff illegally, for such practice was banned, often resorted to using improvised restraints with cords, belts and bandages to tie difficult patients to beds and chairs.

Miss T told of a practice on Ward C of 'pillowing.' A canvas pillowcase had been made with a head hole cut in the closed end and a cord affixed at the open end. If a child became too difficult, self-injured or aggressive, the pillowcase was pulled over his torso and secured, thereby restraining his arms and hands. There were two such pillowcases on Ward C. They were generally used on the more difficult children, especially if they self-injured when put in seclusion. My father was mortified to hear the pillowcase had been used on me at least a dozen times in the last month.

The use of the pillowcases were clearly to intimidate and frighten the patients, and Miss T asserted all the children were terrified them. It was a very effective threat to keep order on a ward of twenty vulnerable and extremely disordered children, some of whom were very challenging to manage.

In the same way the Seclusion Room was supposed to be used as little as possible in events of aggression or to safely contain an agitated or disturbed patient until he calmed down. The use of this room should only be ordered by the practitioner, and only by the nurses in an emergency. Instead, at Hospital X the regime in the Children's Unit tended to use the Seclusion Rooms as a form of punishment to frighten the patients. They should *never* be used time and time again, for many hours at a time, which, said Miss T, was precisely what was happening to me.

Finally, Miss T told my horrified father and his lawyer that Dr Roberts had ordered three leucotomies in the last year. Admittedly they had been very difficult – aggressive – patients, but the treatment had been devastating. One was now mute, and all three left very impaired.

By the time Miss T had concluded giving her evidence, had read and signed her statement as taken down by my father's lawyer, it was eleven o'clock, and everyone was mentally wrung-out by some of the harrowing details of Miss T's evidence. My father had known things were amiss at Hospital X, but he'd had no idea they were as bad as this. This was more a matter for a formal Parliamentary Committee of Enquiry, and it had the potential to devastate the newly formed Welsh Health Authority.

My Dad *knew* he had to get me out of Hospital X as quickly as possible. He knew he now had enough ammunition to cause a major headache for the Secretary of State, unless he bought my father's silence by rescinding my Treatment Order and releasing me to be treated back in a proper psychiatric hospital. Everyone has a price, and that was my father's price for his silence. If the top men of the government would not agree to his terms, he would release the dossier he had complied to the Press, and devastate the Ministry of Health and the Welsh Health Authority.

Even as my father showed his lawyer and Miss T to the front door, even as he sat down in the middle of the night to read Miss T's statement again and began to mentally compose the devastating report he intended to write, my Dad knew he need an extra ace in his pack of cards to force Dr Roberts to abandon his planned leucotomy, and gain my release from Hospital X.

My father had once been an official within Foreign Office intelligence, and his career had spanned from 1954 to 1968, with a return to duty from 1973 to 1974. In short, my father was one of the few men who knew where many of the Cold War skeletons were buried. He had secrets locked in his head – secrets he could *prove* – that could rock the Foreign Office to its very foundations and topple the British government. Yes, my father thought that night, and many years later told me, he would have to produce a skeleton from its grave and make a few top men in Whitehall sweat. My father knew it was a high-risk strategy. He would only be able to fire one arrow, and it had to hit the target first time. He also knew that in firing his arrow he would be forever closing an avenue of employment behind him. He would never again be trusted with a government secret.

Over that February weekend my father wrote a fifty-page report for the eyes of the Secretary of State, David Ennals. It was a detailed and harrowing report, supported by a selection of photographs Miss T had taken with his Minox camera. The report catalogued many abuses and examples of malpractice taking place at Hospital X, and it was a document that would certainly have caused a scandal had it became public knowledge. My father concluded his report by stating he had faith in the National Health Service to be able to rectify these shortcomings internally. My father then wrote a powerful letter to David Ennals that emphasised a different message. He told him of the public outcry that would arise were it to become known that these vulnerable patients were being mistreated and abused, and their relatives would demand a parliamentary enquiry. It was a very potent threat. His letter in effect said: 'Order the leucotomy halted and transfer my son out of Hospital X, or else.' The report was sent off to London by courier on the Monday morning.

Simultaneous to writing his lengthy report on Hospital X, my father composed a long letter to Sir John Hunt, the Cabinet Secretary.

My father had met Sir John two years before when he had started to undertake secret diplomatic work for the Israeli government as an emissary to the Egyptian leader, President Sadat. Sir John had asked my father to a meeting in London, and there explained to him the very delicate nature of his work. He was a free agent to work for the Israelis, sure, but he must make it clear to all parties that he did not represent the British government in any form. After all, Sir John had commented: 'we would not wish to antagonise the oil producing nations.' This meant, of course, that while secretly supporting the Israelis, the British government was mindful that it must remain on good terms with the Arabs for fear of losing access to cheap oil Britain needed so badly in the 1970s.

I suppose the closest analogy I can think of when it comes to how my father felt for me would be a lioness defending her cub to the death. My father therefore decided upon a bold strategy to protect me, but he would set the bridge afire behind him as he went. If his plan failed he could not go back, and for certain I'd be given the leucotomy and remain a damaged mental hospital inmate for the rest of my days.

My father sat down on Sunday night and wrote a careful letter to Sir John Hunt. In his letter he explained his predicament with regard to me. He stated he would not allow me to be operated upon, and he wanted me out of Hospital X. He informed Sir John that he had documents on the Soviet invasion of Hungary in 1956 that proved secret British support for Imre Nagy, the Hungarian Prime Minister, had been an expedient to precipitate an East-West crisis in Europe with the Soviets as a means of distracting world attention from the Suez Crisis, when Britain had invaded Egypt to seize the Suez Canal and tried to topple President Nasser. That revelation was devastating. It had the potential to damage the special relationship with the Americans. But my father went further. He wrote, in clear and concise terms, that unless the Treatment Order was rescinded, on Tuesday, 1 March, he would give a Press conference and announce to the world that he was the secret emissary of the Israelis to the Egyptians. The result would cause considerable damage to Anglo-Arab relations, cost the British economy many millions of pounds in lost trade, and twenty years of goodwill.

The letter to Sir John went off with the courier the same day as the dossier to David Ennals.

Having lit the blue touch paper, my father now sat back and awaited the explosion. He was not in any way complacent. The big question was whether a few top people in Whitehall would think he was bluffing, or was a child locked away in a mental hospital in South Wales going to cost James Callaghan his Premiership and the British government it's standing and good name on the world stage? Was Peter Sinclair going to damage Anglo-Arab relations, indeed Anglo-American relations too, and cost the British economy many millions of pounds for the sake of his thirteen-year-old son?

My father spent the next week living on his nerves. He abandoned any notion of going to work. He contrived to visit me briefly every other afternoon, wondering every time if these were the last days my personality would be intact. Would I soon be mute and impaired, never to talk again? My father did not stay with me very long, for he was maintaining a daily vigil at the telephone, waiting for that so yearned for phone call from someone in London to say if and when I was to be saved.

My father waited all Tuesday, but no call came. He waited all Wednesday, but no call. Surely, he thought, on Thursday, he would hear something, but no. By Friday my father was quite desperate, chain smoking all day whilst he sat reading a copy of Dennis Wheatley's *The Second Seal*. There was no phone call; no letter in the post. My father was quite frantic by now, for with the coming of the weekend he knew no one worked. He spent an hour with me on Saturday and an hour with me on Sunday.

By now the accumulation of weeks of being force-fed and injected with strong drugs had rendered me semi-mute and cabbage-like in the extreme. On the occasions when I now spoke it was just in monosyllable and incoherent.

My father knew I was due to be given the leucotomy in less than forty-eight hours. Was no one going to respond to his report and letters?

On Monday my father resumed his vigil by the telephone and, with nothing else to do, began reading *The Second Seal* once again. It was something to do, but his mind was preoccupied thinking of me. Was I currently in seclusion again? Had I been beaten the night before and spent the night cold, shivering and terrified in the Shower Room? His heart ached for me.

My father's vigil had been going for two hours and he had just made himself a cup of coffee, when the doorbell rang. My father roused himself, hoping that perhaps the post had brought some news. However, instead of the postman my father opened the door to a find tall man in a bowler hat and Crombie overcoat.

This man looks official, thought my father.

The man introduced himself as Mr Tomkinson, and announced he had been sent by Sir John Hunt, the Cabinet Secretary.

My father invited the man in and showed him into the drawing room.

My father and Mr Tomkinson sat quietly for a few moments, until the stranger felt perhaps he ought to start the conversation.

'Sir John read your letter with much interest, Mr Sinclair,' he said. 'He is truly sorry to hear of the plight of young Alex.'

'Yes, it's a terrible worry to me,' replied my father. 'I'm sure with alternate treatment my son is capable of recovery.'

'I don't know anything about that,' replied the man briskly. 'I'm here about your letter to Sir John and your report to Mr Ennals.'

Ah, thought my father, so there has been progress. He decided to play hard-ball back to Tomkinson.

'So,' said my father, 'what's the answer? Is my son to be discharged or am I going to have to go to the Press?'

Mr Tomkinson looked taken aback at having the table turned on him. He'd no doubt imagined he'd find my father a nervous wreck, threatening all sorts of retribution, but quite incapable of carrying it out.

'Now, Mr Sinclair, there is no need to be so hasty,' he said. 'Sir John has told me he is sure an amicable solution can be found.'

'No deal,' my father replied. 'I have the information. I have the documents. Unless the treatment order is rescinded, I go to the Press tomorrow morning. And for everyone's sake, Mr Tomkinson, I promise you I'm not bluffing.'

'I can see that there is little point in discussing the matter further, Mr Sinclair,' said Tomkinson. 'We strongly suggest you reconsider your idea of going to the Press. On the one hand it would be bad for British prestige, and on the other hand I would remind you that the Welsh Health Authority is a new organisation, and your report will cause a lot of damage. I would also remind you that as a former diplomat of the Political Intelligence Division you are subject to the Official Secrets Act, and we will prosecute you if you reveal details of your work in 1956.'

'I don't care if you prosecute me,' my father stated. 'By the time you do that, I will have brought the government crashing down.'

'I can see there is no negotiating with you, Mr Sinclair. If you are determined on this course of action you will cause an international crisis.'

'Do I get my deal?' pressed my father.

Mr Tomkinson nodded. 'Yes, you get your "deal." Mr Ennals has requested a review of the child's treatment, with a change of emphasis.'

And with that Mr Tomkinson stood up to leave.

'Is that all?' my father asked. 'Is there nothing more to be said?'

'Yes, that's all. There is nothing more to be said.' Tomkinson broke into a weak smile for the first time. 'I think you bested your own government, Mr Sinclair. I hope your son will now get treatment of the kind you desire. I would venture to suggest, however, that you never threaten the Cabinet Secretary again. It would be most unwise.'

'Yes,' my father replied.

Mr Tomkinson paused at the door.

'Oh, there is just one more thing,' he said. 'I'll take that file of documents you have on the Hungarian Crisis, if you don't mind. That's *our* price.'

'Okay,' my father responded. 'It's a fair deal, just so long as Sir John keeps his promise.'

'Mr Sinclair!' Tomkinson replied indignantly. 'I assure you the British government *always* keeps its promises!'

My father's car revved high as he raced along the main road to the hospital. It was Monday lunchtime, and just one hour after his curious meeting with Mr Tomkinson. As he drove his mind was full of all the possibilities for me. Of key significance to my father was had Dr Roberts yet been told the leucotomy order had been rescinded? Would he agree to transfer me out of Ward C? Might he even decide to transfer me to a different hospital? My Dad swung in though the hospital gates and skidded the car to a halt in the car park.

My father later told me he felt as if he walked on air that lunchtime. He had just had a meeting with a top government official, and in the rarefied atmosphere of Whitehall someone had decided to take a direct decision on my behalf to protect my future rights to thrive or fall on my own account. What happened to me now in hospital care was going to be down to me to prove myself capable of recovery. Please do not think, however, that my father was a man who lived with his head in the clouds. He knew that he would have to be hard on me now to force me to grasp my problems and fight to get better.

As my father entered the Children's Unit Dr Roberts suddenly appeared as if he had been waiting for him, and asked him into his office.

As my father took a seat, Dr Roberts shuffled his papers on his desk nervously.

'Er, Mr Sinclair,' Dr Roberts began, 'I've a late change of heart with regards to young Alex.'

'Oh, yes,' my father replied.

'Yes. I am sure his condition is chronic, but it would be unsympathetic and wrong to completely discount the possibilities that he might make a partial recovery. Please bear in mind that autism is a life-long condition, but perhaps some form of alternate treatment would alleviate some of the more devastating results of his psychotic illness.'

'Yes.'

'I have therefore decided, just this morning in fact, to rescind the leucotomy operation scheduled for tomorrow, and recommend psychiatric treatment instead.'

'Here?' my father asked.

'Oh, no,' Dr Roberts said hastily. 'No, I've recommended a transfer of Alex back to Pen-y-Fal Hospital. They will work with you there and give every opportunity to see if Alex is capable of some sort of recovery. If he can recover, all well and good. Personally I don't believe he will ever recover, but we'll give it a month, just a month, after which I hope you realise he will have to come back here.

Alex is to be sent back to Pen-y-Fal tomorrow morning. The arrangements have already been made.'

My father stood up to leave, and had just reached the door when Dr Roberts hissed at him: 'Just how did you manage to interfere with my treatment of your son?'

My father paused at the door. 'Your treatment of my son is the least of your worries,' he replied. 'I've made a full report on you and your methods, Dr Roberts, and the abuses conducted at this hospital, to the Secretary of State himself. You can expect a thorough inspection anytime soon.' And with that he slammed the door behind him.

Twenty minutes later my father was sat in the Visiting Room when I was brought in by a nurse.

In an instant my father was across the room and giving me a huge hug.

'I've moved heaven and earth for you, Alex,' he said with a lump in his throat. 'Don't you dare let me down, son. Not now. Now you've got to get better. Now there is no choice.'

CHAPTER 5

# Love

The snow spread like a duvet of neat crisp folds over cars, shrubs and the little nineteenth century pavilion viewed across the lawn in the distance. A flurry in late March had transformed the brick buildings of Pen-y-Fal Hospital temporarily into a winter wonderland.

'Do you like snow, Alex?' Judy asked, as I stood in my dressing-gown gazing out of my bedroom window.

'Yes,' I said, giving Judy a rare smile. 'I love snow.'

I turned my gaze back to the glaring white beyond my window. There was even an inch of snow on the sill beyond my locked window. So close but yet so far, I thought. Snow and I had only ever had a passing acquaintance, for I'd spent most of my childhood living in Cornwall, where the sea is warmed by the Gulf Stream making the climate sub-tropical. Even frost had been a rarity. It was a novel experience for me to see so much snow.

Yes, I thought again for the umpteenth time that morning, so close but yet so far.

I had been back at Pen-y-Fal three weeks. I had arrived back on Tuesday, 2 March, clad only in a soiled diaper, all-in-one, and wrapped in a blanket. I was bruised all over, and Hospital X had shorn my hair to a crew-cut. I had lost a lot of weight and was skeletal. I couldn't even talk coherently anymore. Everyone was horrified at my condition, and Judy's eyes had filled with tears at the sight of me.

Once back at Pen-y-Fal my father had been a regular visitor, and he had many meetings with Dr Jones. He was a worried man. Was my catastrophic collapse permanent? Would I fail to respond to treatment and be sent back to Hospital X again, this time for good?

To start with, my father told me many years later, Dr Jones was not best pleased to find himself responsible for me again. He saw me as disturbed and a disruption on the ward.

'Please understand, Mr Sinclair,' Dr Jones told my father, 'a lot is going to be up to Alex. There can be no more edging around his mental frailties. He's going to have to confront the past, reconcile it to his life now, and I'm going to work him very hard.'

'Yes, I understand,' my father had replied. 'You must do whatever's necessary to restore him to health. As you know, his mother nearly killed him in her hatred of him. That took its toll. But maybe I'm as much to blame for being too soft with him. I should have been firmer the moment his mental aberrations started when he was eight-years-old. And now he's been reduced to a terrible state, and I'm not sure if he'll ever recover.'

'I know you have reservations about invasive treatments,' Dr Jones had responded, 'but I now believe Alex's mental disorder, though virulent, is rooted deep down in a depressive psychosis. I'm therefore going to schedule him for a course of Electro Convulsive Therapy straight away, twelve doses over the next four weeks. I am mindful that when we gave Alex ECT a year ago he suffered a number of epileptic events, but the treatment worked and he got better. I therefore have to weigh the balance between the advantages of cure, against the disadvantages of disorder.

'I see from his notes that when he left us in January, Dr Roberts withdrew treatment by Haloperidol, and his drug regime since then has primarily been the barbiturate Sodium Amytal, and sedatives. This was, in my opinion, unwise. High doses of Sodium Amytal impairs the receptor cells in the brain lessening agitation in the patient, but at the same time repeated use will diminish the electrical activity in the brain which manifests as incoherence, such as we now see in Alex. In long term use the toxic effects can become permanent. Dr Roberts states in his notes this treatment was necessary because Alex became violent.'

The fact that I'd been taken off therapeutic Haloperidol and instead been drugged up to the eyeballs with barbiturate was news to my father, and he wondered if that was the reason I had become increasingly incoherent and impaired at Hospital X.

'Most unfortunate,' continued Dr Jones. 'I will stop the barbiturate and immediately reinstate the Haloperidol, and give him the maximum dose for a time. I cannot maintain it indefinitely, however, because he might develop tardive dyskinesia, a movement disorder caused by high doses of the drug.'

My father gave Dr Jones his full support for whatever kind of treatments would work. There were just two avenues open now: either cure and recovery, or failure and a chronically sick son sent back to Hospital X.

Over the next three weeks, taken off the sedatives and barbiturate, and put on the maximum dose of Haloperidol, I began to wake from my nightmare world, and eventually my mind began to function again. However, for the first week I suffered paradoxical delirium, and ironically had to be sedated to keep me quiet. Thereafter I began to talk again, and was somewhat coherent, though limited in my scope of conversation. Evidently the Haloperidol worked.

By taking me off the antipsychotic and dosing me with barbiturate, Hospital X had done me more harm than good. Indeed, given another few days in that place they would have operated on my brain and ruined my life... forever.

'Would you like to go outside for a walk in the snow?' Judy asked me.

I can so clearly remember, all these years later, that my eyes went like saucers at the prospect of being allowed outside.

'Oh, pl... please. Can I?' I stammered, almost pleading.

'I'm sure it's possible,' Judy said with a smile. 'But you'll have to promise to stay calm and do as I say.'

I nodded in eager anticipation of a wonderful adventure to come. My heartbeat quickened in anticipation.

I was told to get dressed and put my coat on. Judy found a pair of Wellington boots for me, slightly too big so I slopped about in them, and before I knew it I was walking hand in hand with her in the direction of the quaint little wooden pavilion on the far side of the hospital grounds.

The air was chill on my face, cold in my lungs, and everything had a wonderful clean smell. Judy wore a thick nurse's cape over her anorak, its broad red straps crossing her chest. She paused to adjust her cape, letting go of my hand.

Freedom! I thought, reaching out to a bush to grasp a handful of snow. I let it fall in sprinkles from my fingers.

Judy put an arm about my shoulders.

'Come on,' she said. 'To the pavilion and back, and then we'll have a hot chocolate.'

Judy urged me on, her conversation endearing.

Then, to my delight, it started to snow. Not very heavily, just enough to muffle sound and give the illusion of rising from the ground.

I stopped walking and lifted my head back as far as it would go until I was staring skyward and could feel the delicious sensation of snowflakes landing on my eyelids and lips. I let the flakes land on my tongue.

Nikki would have loved this, I thought.

I started, shocked that the thought had leapt unbidden into my mind. I had tried to stop thinking of Nikki, but the more I tried the worse it got.

Suddenly I was no longer smiling in the snow. I was crying, distraught with ice-cold tears running down my face.

'Oh, sweet pea!' Judy exclaimed. 'Whatever's the matter?'

'It's Nikki,' I sobbed. 'I want Nikki.'

'But he's no longer here, dear,' Judy replied gently.

Judy, indeed all the nurses on my ward, had been told the tragic story of Nikki, knew how he had died, knew I pined for him.

'But I want him back,' I sobbed. 'I killed him; it was my fault.'

'No,' said Judy firmly. 'It was *not* your fault. Now come on Alex, try to be strong.'

'But it's my fault he died,' I insisted.

'Now I'm sure that's not true,' Judy responded. 'Do you want to talk about it?' she asked, as we continued on our way to the pavilion.

We sat on a dry seat and I kicked at the snow in my loose-fitting boots.

'Now what happened?' Judy asked.

I decided to open up to one of the few people in the world I trusted. I couldn't tell my father, not yet. He wouldn't understand. I started to talk, to tell Judy things I had never even discussed with Dr Schultz.

'When I was committed in the terrible asylum in Greece, I made friends with Nikki, who was epileptic. I told Nikki I was sure my Dad would rescue me, and I promised to get him out too; then we'd have a happy life together and live like brothers. The trouble was I couldn't speak Greek, and Nikki spoke no English, so we were unable to talk to each other. But bad things can happen, and what was to happen next was my fault.'

I stifled a sob, and Judy put her arm around my shoulders.

'When you're ready, dear,' she said.

'One day I misbehaved, and this resulted in Nikki and I being dragged away and flung into an isolation cell together. The last time I'd been sent to isolation, I spent two days there before being returned to the ward. The two orderlies on the ward were furious with me, and beat me with a belt causing me deep cuts on my bottom and thighs. They then put a restraint on my waist and wrists, and flung me naked and bleeding into a cell where I remained locked up all alone like an animal for a fortnight.'

I was crying openly by now, the trauma of reliving the ordeal about as much as I could cope with.

'Go on,' said Judy.

'Well, on the day I was locked in isolation cell with Nikki, I was terrified by the thought of what the orderlies would do to me this time. I just stared at the locked door and cried my eyes out. Then Nikki turned me to face him. He was laughing, seeing this as a great adventure.

'"Stop it!" I shouted. "Don't you realise what's going to happen to me now." And with that I pushed Nikki to stop him laughing. Nikki pushed me back. I retaliated by shoving him in the chest, so Nikki shoved me back. In moments we were rolling around on the floor, fighting. I was smaller than Nikki, but I managed to get on top of him and sat on his chest, trying to calm him down, but he fought back all the time.'

I began to sob hysterically, almost unable to go on.

'Suddenly Nikki spasmed,' I said. 'He suffered an epileptic fit far worse than I'd ever seen him suffer on the ward. He flailed about. He whimpered. He peed on the floor. I tried to hold Nikki to me, to protect him from hurting himself, but he was thrashing about too violently to hold still. Then Nikki began to make a choking sound, and when I looked in his mouth I saw he'd swallowed his tongue. Then he died. It was my fault we'd ended up in isolation. If we'd still been on the ward, the orderlies would have known how to save him. It was my fault we fought. Nikki's death was my fault. I killed him.'

At this I broke down into sobs of anguish and trauma.

Judy cuddled me as I wept on and on, perhaps for quarter an hour.

Judy sat silently for a very long time, and I thought that perhaps I'd made a terrible mistake in telling her what had happened. I looked up into her face.

Tears were running down her cheeks, and she looked at me sadly.

'Oh, Alex,' she said finally, 'is this what you have to live with?'

I nodded.

'You'll have to tell Dr Jones, you know.'

'No, no,' I cried in panic. 'I don't want him to know. He'll think me a bad person, and then he'll never let me go.'

'It won't be like that, Alex,' Judy responded kindly. 'You were a victim, just like Nikki. Dr Jones *has* to know. Then he'll understand you better, and be better able to make you well again.'

I began to cry again, both for Nikki and my fear of Dr Jones.

I nodded my head, my tears continuing to fall. Nodding my head to Judy was one thing, believing was quite another.

With that Judy abandoned the idea of sitting at the pavilion to look at the snow, and we got up to return. I could feel her firmer grip on my arm, the sudden urgency in her quickened steps. The beauty of the snow faded, for now instead of a walk in the park-like grounds, the beauty of bushes and little shrubs in the snow, ahead of me lay the austere barrack-like nineteenth century red-brick buildings of a mental hospital.

I sobbed all the way back to the ward, arm in arm with Judy as she hurried me back to a place of safety with other nurses to help her in case I became difficult again.

I am sure my father loved me deeply, even if he was a very reserved sort of man to rarely, if ever, actually said it. My father had been through hell to rescue me from Greece. He had then been given back a child who'd gone insane, and I mean real screaming insanity of the worst sort, whom he'd taken back to West Germany and paid a lot of money to get me treated by one of the top psychiatrists in the country.

Outwardly restored to health, we'd returned to Britain, where my father bought a large house near my grandmother's home in a leafy suburb of Cardiff.

We were very close, the two of us. He took me for days out in the car. He took me rowing on Cardiff's Roath Lake, and every Saturday morning he took me to the nearby seaside town of Penarth where he bought me a huge dessert of tinned fruit, a whole banana, topped by ice-cream and a cherry. I'd sit with a long spoon, gazing out of the window at the sea, eating my treat whilst my father sat sipping his coffee, talking about all sorts of things, from Queen Cleopatra to the different types of birdsong he knew. I always sat and listened, for I loved my Dad and had the sort of enquiring mind that liked to listen. However, and it is a big however, my father was not the sort of man who'd ever discuss anything emotional. He would not talk about my mother, at least not to me, and he'd never say he loved me. I just had to take it on trust that he did. We were a very proper upright pair of father and son, very middle class, he in a sports jacket and cravat, me always tidily dressed. But as we walked in the street, though he would often place a hand on my shoulder or take my arm to cross the street, that was about as affectionate as it ever got. If I got overly affectionate and hugged him in the street, tried to playfully tickle him at home, he'd draw himself up stiffly and tell me to stop it.

One day towards the end of March, about a week after it snowed, Dr Jones wanted to see me and my father together. I had now finished my first course of ECT, and I had been on the maximum dose of Haloperidol for nearly a month. However, I just did not seem to be getting better in the right direction. My screaming fits and self-injury were now a rarity, and at least I was cognitive again, but in psychiatric terms I was a real mess. I just would not accept that I wasn't responsible for my grandmother and Nikki's deaths, and I had developed very fixated – paranoid – beliefs that Dr Jones found hard to challenge.

Dr Jones had by now confronted me about the death of Nikki, which I'd confided to Judy, but I'd refused to talk about my experience to him, and he thought I was being difficult and paranoid. He seemed less concerned about my painful and horrible memories, and more concerned by my current mental state. However, to help me get over the trauma of Nikki's death, he decided to organise a series of consultations for me with the Unit Psychotherapist, Mr Reese.

My primary delusion at present was that my Dad hated me, and I'd shed bitter tears whenever Dr Jones tried to get me to talk about it. I claimed he'd put me in hospital to get rid of me (it would be many years before I learnt the truth about Hospital X) and, rather insanely, I claimed people were poisoning my food.

This last delusion was most bizarre, I have to admit, and the only way the nurses on the ward could cope was to give me the first choice off the trolley of breakfast, lunch and tea. Even then I would only pick at my food, and I was by now primarily existing on a diet of apples and bananas. For some bizarre reason I didn't think fruit could be poisoned. And why did I think my food was poisoned? Well, I was sure somewhere behind the scenes I was the victim of an evil plot to keep me locked up in hospital and kill me. In psychiatric terms this would be called a paranoid delusion, and Dr Jones was very puzzled if not a little perturbed, because such paranoia is rare in children.

Dr Jones had already decided to give me a second course of ECT over the coming month, but he wanted to try something first. He wanted to see father and son interact in the quiet of the Visiting Room, with himself present as mediator. He decided this because in my less lucid moments I had told the nurses I blamed my father for some of the bad things that had happened to me because he didn't love me. I blamed him for allowing my mother to abuse me as a child. I blamed him for sticking me in St Lawrence's Hospital for five months when I was nine-years-old. I blamed him for leaving me in the Attica for seven months and not rescuing me until it was almost too late. I blamed him for sending me to Hospital X. Indeed, I had Schultz's 'voice' telling me this was so, so it must be true I said. I knew if I showed any sort of physical affection towards my father he would go all stiff and withdrawn, just like my mother, as if affection from me was repellent and to be avoided. My mother had hated me all my life and even tried to kill me. It was therefore not a great leap of the imagination for me, a mentally fragile child, to compare the withdrawn nature of my father to that of my mother, and I knew she didn't love me, she had told me often enough.

And so it was that one Friday afternoon in March, Nurse Johnson took me downstairs to the Visiting Room. On seeing my Dad I flew across the room and gave him a hug, whilst he remained rather stiff and formal. Then I realised Dr Jones was in the room, and I was immediately suspicious something nasty was about to happen.

'Alex,' said Dr Jones, breaking into a rare smile, 'sit next to your father. I want to talk to you both.'

My Dad sat in an easy chair. I sat next to him.

'Alex, why do you think people hate you?' asked Dr Jones.

'I'm a bad person,' I replied. 'People die when I like them. Do you know I made a friend in Greece called Nikki who died when I...'

'Now stop it, Alex,' Dr Jones cut it. 'We're not going to talk about Nikki today.'

I fell silent.

'Alex,' said my father. 'Why have you been telling Dr Jones and the nurses that I don't like you? That's a very cruel thing to say, you know.'

I now realised that when I thought I had said something in confidence to Judy, Nurse Clark, or even Dr Jones, it must have all been written in my notes. My own words were now going to be used as a weapon against me. I could feel my tears welling up and I began to tremble.

Not now, I thought. Don't cry and show weakness. Not now!

'Everyone hates me,' I said. 'People hate me for killing Nikki and Nanny, and they are poisoning my food. I have to live on fruit and I...'

'This is all nonsense, Alex,' my Dad interrupted, a hint of anger in his voice. 'No one hates you. You haven't killed anyone. And no one is poisoning your food.'

'Tell me, Alex,' said Dr Jones, 'surely you know your father loves you.'

Annoyingly my tears began to run freely, and my trembling was becoming worse. It wasn't a normal tremble. Little electric shocks were running up and down my arms and legs that made them twitch and jump, and it was getting worse.

'Oh, Dad...' I started to say, then I passed out.

When I came to I was lying on my side on the floor, and Dr Jones and my father were holding me.

'It's okay, Alex.' Dr Jones was saying calmly. 'It's okay, now.'

Apparently I had suffered petit mal (a mild epileptic-type seizure with a brief loss of consciousness) which I was suffering as a side-effect of the ECT.

My father was holding my hand.

'Alex,' he said gently. 'Oh, Alex, are you okay?"

I was helped up off the floor and sat on a chair.

'Mr Sinclair,' said Dr Jones. 'I think there is something you have to say to Alex, and you know what it is.'

My father knelt before me as I sat trembling in my seat. He put his arms around me and drew me into an embrace, a rare tender embrace.

'Alex,' he said. 'I love you very much. You mean the entire world to me, and I will always be there for you. I love you more than anyone else in this world.'

'Oh, Dad,' I exclaimed, returning his embrace. 'I love you too.'

'Alex,' interrupted Dr Jones, 'I think we've made some progress this afternoon. You know your father loves you, and you love your father. I don't want to hear any more talk that people don't like you or hate you, and I don't want to hear any more talk that you've killed people.'

I nodded my head, knowing my father's love was genuine. As to whether other people hated me, or that I got people killed, well, I wasn't willing to confront Dr Jones. There would be plenty of time ahead for me, and for him, to find out whether or not this was true.

Following my March meeting with my father, Dr Jones took several decisions. One was to remove me from the seclusion of my single room and place me in one of the six-bed dormitories. The other was that there would be no more pandering to my delusions and aberrations.

Every second day during April, a nurse took me downstairs to the Treatment Room after lunch. Here I'd lie on a trolley, straps over my chest and knees to keep me safe. I'd receive an injection to make me sleep for ten minutes, at which point I'd receive the ECT, Dr Jones placing electrodes on my temples and give my brain an electric shock. This was Electro-Convulsive Therapy in its refined form of 1977. Then, following my treatment, I'd be taken, confused and muddle-headed, back to my dormitory to sleep the afternoon away. Regrettably ECT, regardless of the benefits, impairs the mind for twenty-four hours, and I regularly found myself asking what day it was? What were the nurses' names? Why was I having to stay in bed?

The second major decision Dr Jones took was that he was going to supplement the Haloperidol with a drug called Methotrimeprazine, given by injection. Both Haloperidol and Methotrimeprazine were primarily drugs for the treatment of schizophrenia, but they had value in the management of psychosis. Unfortunately Methotrimeprazine is quite sedating, so to start with I was very sleepy all the time, so sleepy in fact that the nurses were often able to trick me into eating half my meal before I rebelled, claiming it was poisoned and refused to eat any more. It was only then that the nurses would produce apples or bananas for me to eat.

The final decision of Dr Jones was that I should interact with the other boys. Under his care and treatment, and probably due to the medication, I had largely ceased to self-injure. My head-banging tantrums were now a rarity, although I continued to bite my hands when I got agitated or upset. With this newfound mental equilibrium Dr Jones decided that, together with my move to the dormitory, I should now spend all my days in the Day Room, attend morning lessons, have lunch with the other boys and be allowed free-time in the afternoons. This was a major improvement in my life, for I had become terribly lonely spending all my time locked in my room.

It was now that events began to build an unfortunate momentum of their own, and I was in no small way to blame. When I'd been a patient at Pen-y-Fal the previous year, I had made friends with a boy called Mark. Mark was blond and good-looking, but unstable; a sixteen-year-old schizophrenic who had been a patient at Pen-y-Fal for nearly three years. Mark was also a sociopath, which meant he could be violent – dangerous – when he couldn't get his own way. This was to be Mark's last year on Ward 3, for when he became seventeen he would be transferred from the Children's Unit to the main hospital. Because Mark was unstable and dangerous, Judy once told me to be careful what I said to Mark, and confided he'd probably have to stay at Pen-y-Fal, or a supervised unit, all his life.

Regardless of Mark's problems he was often full of fun, and for some reason he liked me. We'd been friends the previous year, and he now ensured we would be friends again. Mark was a full head and shoulders taller than me, and on my first full day in the Day Room he rushed over and gave me a hug. He then introduced me to his latest batch of friends: Nigel, Andy and Mike. Life on Ward 3 meant that the patients came and went with fair regularity. Some would stay a week or two, then be discharged; others, like me, had been sectioned and would stay for three or more months. The only constant on Ward 3 were the nurses, Mrs Howell the teacher, and poor Mark, who saw his friends come and go, and he often felt lonely and abandoned. Mark told me once that his father, who ran a car dealership in Abergavenny, only came to see him once every few months, and he hadn't seen his mother or sister in three years. He was very bitter about that situation.

I now found my days given structure, and attended morning lessons every weekday with Mrs Howell, sat next to Mark at a refectory table. However, just as my days were now organised for me, every second day, after lunch, I had to have my ECT, and I really hated it. I can see in hindsight that I was being treated and cured, but at the time it was not a pleasant experience.

Twice a week I'd have a session with Dr Jones, and he'd ask me all sorts of questions: 'Are you eating your meals now, Alex?' 'Why have you been crying again?' 'Will you explain to me why you believe you've killed people?' 'Have you been hearing voices again?'

Sometimes I'd answer his questions. More often I'd get upset and break into tears and refuse to answer, and Dr Jones would give up in exasperation and send me back to the ward.

Dr Jones and Mr Reese told my father that my delusion that people had died because of me was a huge hurdle, and they weren't quite sure how to defuse this distressing belief, buried deep in my psyche along with the belief that I was worthless and people hated me. Mr Reese had tried every trick he knew to get me to talk about Nikki, and sometimes I'd talk a bit about it, but there was a cut-off point beyond which I wouldn't go. Dr Jones told my father that they'd have to start with a small step and convince me my grandmother was alive and well, and that I hadn't killed her. If he could break that first delusion, then probably the others would come tumbling down too.

My father agreed, but reminded him that when he'd followed Dr Schultz's advice and confronted me with my grandmother in December, I'd suffered a screaming fit and the event had sent me over the edge into a severe breakdown. Dr Jones ventured to suggest that given a little more time perhaps my grandmother could come back to see me, but he'd make sure this time that I was well enough to handle the event, and perhaps he'd even give me a mild sedative before the meeting took place. If they could just break the delusion that people died because of me it would be a major hurdle overcome on my road to recovery.

Best wait until I had completed my last course of ECT, said Dr Jones, then they could consider the situation again.

It was now the middle of April and, having received eight of my twelve doses of ECT, a new problem manifested itself, and it came from an unexpected quarter.

One morning, sat at the table with Mark for a maths lesson given by Mrs Howell, I began to feel lightheaded and strange, and the last thing I remember was my right hand spasmed causing me to drop my pencil. The next thing I knew I was laying on the floor, Mark was in tears, and Nurse Johnson was holding me and telling me I was going to be alright. I could hear the ward alarm ringing. Then Dr Jones appeared at the run.

He assisted Nurse Johnson to get me up off the floor and they took me out of the Day Room to my dormitory, where they sat me on my bed. Dr Jones looked into my eyes with a small pencil torch, then made me squeeze his hand, first with my left hand and then my right.

'I think you're going to be alright, Alex,' Dr Jones said. 'Now just stay calm and lay down for me.'

He turned to Nurse Johnson, and asked her to explain what had happened.

'It was a grand mal, Doctor,' she said. 'A full tonic-colonic seizure; a full epileptic fit. It wasn't just a petit mal this time.'

'I see,' Dr Jones replied. He rubbed his chin in contemplation, before turning back to me.

'Alex,' he said, 'how do you feel?'

'I feel sick and giddy,' I replied. 'Please, Doctor Jones, what's happening to me? Am I going to be alright?'

'Oh, yes,' he said. 'You'll be fine, but I want you to stay in bed for the rest of the morning. You've had a little fit, that's all, so I expect you'll sleep now.'

And with that Dr Jones and Nurse Johnson left me lying on my bed and closed the door on their way out.

However, what had happened to me was no 'little fit.' I'd had a grand mal, not a petit mal like previously. A grand mal is a full epileptic fit in which my brain had short circuited, leaving me unconscious and twitching on the floor in a spasmodic seizure.

As a result of this development Dr Jones abandoned the final doses of ECT. To suffer fits as a result – a side-effect – was an uncommon event. Petit mals could be managed, but grand mals were another thing entirely, and quite serious.

Dr Jones decided that without the use of ECT he would order Mr Reese to practice psychoanalysis on me in thrice weekly sessions. That I was making progress there was no doubt, but I was still a delusional psychotic who needed to be pushed ever forward towards recovery and cure.

Dr Jones was a very clever practitioner, and he would not allow me to languish at Pen-y-Fal. He was quite sure by now that deep within my troubled mind I had the ability to recover. The trick was going to be what strategy he used, and not to cause me to relapse.

'Alex is on the correct medication now,' Dr Jones told my father a few days later. 'I will use no more ECT, for I cannot risk causing him to suffer another epileptic fit, but I'm sure that we just need a little luck, perhaps make him meet his grandmother under controlled circumstances, to set him on the road to a full recovery.'

Dr Jones was a wise man. The only trouble was neither he nor my father could foresee that an event in the future would put all their hard work at risk of failure, and I would have my sanity once again threatened from a completely unexpected source.

As April proceeded so my mental equilibrium seemed to be very slowly restored. However, it was such a slow process that to me life seemed very boring on the Ward. A regulated regime on a locked ward of breakfast at 8:00 a.m., lessons in the morning, lunch at 1:00 p.m., recreation in the afternoon, tea at 5:00 p.m., television in the evening, and bed at precisely 9:30 p.m. Regardless of the nurses' best endeavours to introduce variety, it was a very institutional environment, and there was always the possibility of a disturbance by an unstable boy who'd end up in time-out for an hour or two, and I regret to say the boy was still sometimes me. By mid-April I had been at Pen-y-Fal accumulatively for four and a half months, and I was really pining for my Dad and a change of scenery. By April only Mark and I were the original patients of December.

Every afternoon we boys would watch the television, or play dominoes, Monopoly or Cluedo, which sounds quite fun, but when you've played the same games every afternoon for months on end it became quite monotonous.

With the better weather of April, the nurses tried to bring a little variation into our lives. Twice a week, Nurse Johnson and an escorting auxiliary nurse would take ten boys out for a walk in the hospital grounds, and our destination was the quaint little pavilion, there to sit and chat, stare at the trees, or even play catch with a ball.

By now Dr Jones seemed pleased that I'd been persuaded out of my delusion that evil unseen persons were poisoning my food. That element of cure had been very hard on me, for Dr Jones ordered the nurses to make me stay at the table until I'd eaten all my meals. Initially this was no easy cure, for I'd sobbed and screamed I'd die if I ate the food, shedding bitter tears over every mouthful, and several times ended up in time-out for throwing my food on the floor. As hard and unpleasant as the treatment was, I was helped along by Mark who smiled conspiratorially at me during mealtimes and, when the nurses looked away, quickly swapped his empty plate for my unfinished meal. Thus, despite Dr Jones belief I'd been cured of that delusion, I still got away without having to eat my meals.

It was after one such lunch, when I'd smugly thought I'd got away – with Mark's aid – with not having to eat my meal of lasagne and got up from the table, that Dr Jones appeared on the ward. With a serious expression on his face he asked me to follow him out of the Day Room.

Had my deception been discovered? I wondered.

I looked at Mark who shrugged and pulled a face.

'Alex,' called Dr Jones, 'come on. I haven't got all day.'

'Sorry, Doctor,' I replied, and followed him out into the corridor. He paused at the Ward Office, said a few words to Nurse Johnson, and produced a yellow tablet for me to take with a glass of water.

I took the tablet, then Dr Jones directed me to follow him down the corridor. He unlocked the ward door, and I followed him downstairs to his office.

Once in his office, Dr Jones told me to sit before him. I was still fearful that my mealtime deception had been discovered and was about to get into trouble. I fiddled with my hands in my lap as Dr Jones talked, but I wasn't listening.

'Alex!' said Dr Jones, and I started. 'Haven't you been listening to me?'

'I'm sorry, Doctor Jones,' I replied.

Dr Jones looked exasperated.

'Okay,' he said. 'Now listen. You've been having sessions with Mr Reese three times a week for the last month. You've talked through your problems, haven't you?'

'Yes, Doctor.'

'Good. I have been looking after you for four months, so you trust me, don't you?'

'Yes, Doctor.'

'Good.' Dr Jones leaned forward on his desk. 'Now I want to talk to you about your grandmother.'

'I killed her,' I stated. 'I didn't mean to, but I...'

'Now stop, Alex,' Dr Jones interrupted me. 'All this talk of deaths is no good. You've never killed anyone, and today I'm going to prove it to you.'

I began to tremble in fear of what Dr Jones was going to do. I sat nervously upon my hands and began to look wildly about Dr Jones's office.

Dr Jones got up and went to the door, opened it, and said: 'Come in please.'

I squirmed around, and was surprised to see my Dad and Judy enter the room.

'Hello, Alex,' my father said.

'Hi, Dad,' I replied.

'Now, Alex,' Dr Jones continued, 'why do you believe you killed your granny?'

'Because I made her have a heart attack, and I saw the ambulance take her dead body away.'

'Nanny didn't die, Alex,' said my father. 'She had a heart attack, yes. But she got better.'

'No!' I declared. 'She died.'

'No, she did not,' said Dr Jones, 'and I'm going to prove that to you now, this very moment.'

He went back to the door, opened it and went out. I could hear him talking.

'Alex,' said my father, 'I've brought Nanny here to meet you this afternoon.'

'No, no,' I cried, leaping from my seat and rushing into Judy's arms. 'Please don't do this to me, Dad,' I sobbed. 'Please, please, don't do this.'

Suddenly the door was opening.

I turned my face into Judy, held her tight and shut my eyes. I was crying in anguish by now.

'Alex,' said a lady's voice gently. 'Alex, won't you turn and talk to me?'

I felt a hand on my shoulder.

Still crying in anguish, despite the Valium (the yellow tablet), I slowly turned to face the lady.

There, to my absolute astonishment, and looking very healthy, stood my grandmother in a smart overcoat and hat, her hair neatly done, her makeup smelling of Rose Geranium.

I was still crying, but now I was crying for joy as I let go of Judy and turned to embrace my grandmother. I held her tight, taking in the scent of her, and feeling her warm cheek against mine as she gave me a kiss.

Everything happened quite quickly now, for a satisfied Dr Jones directed Judy to take me and my grandmother to the Visiting Room across the corridor, while he continued to talk to my father.

For the next half hour I was allowed to sit with my grandmother, and my heart leapt for joy to find her alive and well, and not, as I'd thought for the last five months, dead and gone.

I chatted happily, telling her about my friends on the ward, and she told me she was looking forward to when I was well enough to come home, 'home' to live with her. Once my half hour was up, Dr Jones and my father came in, and Dad promised to bring my grandmother back for another visit one day.

With that, a hug and a kiss, and a cheerful wave to my grandmother, Judy took me back to the ward, and I had a bounce in my step as I talked excitedly to Judy about my granny.

Once back in the ward, I ran into the Day Room to seek out my friends.

As I ran in I spotted Mark standing by the television. He looked up as I ran over to him.

'My granny's alive! My granny's alive!' I exclaimed excitedly. 'Oh, I'm so happy, Mark. I'm so happy. I love everyone. I love you too.' And with that I gave Mark a hug.

To my astonishment Mark hugged me back and kissed my cheek.

Before I knew what was happening Mark was running across the Day Room to Nurse Johnson and Judy.

'Alex loves me!' he shouted. 'Alex loves me! Someone in this world loves me for just being me! Oh, I'm so happy...' And with that he began to dance around the room getting very overexcited.

Judy rushed over to me.

'Whatever did you say to Mark?' she demanded, a hint of anger in her voice I'd never heard before. 'I warned you he was unstable. I told you to be careful. Why, oh why, didn't you listen to me?'

'Alex loves me!' Mark continued to sing as if in a rhyme.

I watched Mark leaping and dancing around the Day Room, and wondered if I hadn't made a most terrible, if unwitting, mistake.

# CHAPTER 6

# Fate

In the present day a child with moderately severe mental problems, including psychosis, would probably be treated at home under the modern concept of 'care in the community.' Indeed, with the closure of so many mental hospitals in Britain in recent years it would probably be near impossible to admit any but the most dire cases to psychiatric care. However, back in 1977 the psychiatry service in Britain was still properly run, still properly funded, still properly resourced, and this meant that a child such as I was lucky enough to be properly treated. Pen-y-Fal was an excellent hospital, run by excellent doctors, excellent staff nurses and excellent nursing auxiliaries. Thus, in a way, despite the fact I had been so ill and now yearned to go home, by the middle of April it was comforting and reassuring to know I was in safe hands.

My meeting and re-familiarisation with my grandmother took place on Tuesday, 12 April. After months of endeavour and steady progress, Dr Jones had managed to make me confront my delusion that I'd killed my grandmother, and thus a very important step had been taken on my road to recovery. My father was naturally overjoyed at this significant step and thought I had made such good progress, compared to my screaming insanity and self-injury of the previous December, that he could soon take me home. However, my father, diplomat and expert on international politics though he was, was no medical man, so perhaps not unnaturally he was mistaken.

Many years later, my father told me what had happened when he met with Dr Jones on the morning of Friday, 15 April.

My father asked if and when he could take me home, imagining Dr Jones was going to say 'next week' or 'in a fortnight.'

Instead of a smile and encouraging words, Dr Jones, with a dour face and a shake of his head, immediately disillusioned my father.

'No,' he said. 'Alex is still far from well, despite the success with his grandmother last Tuesday. I'm afraid we're certainly talking of many weeks yet, if not months.'

'Surely not!' exclaimed my father. 'Alex is so much better now. He doesn't suffer screaming fits anymore. He now knows he didn't kill his grandmother, and he is so much like the boy I used to know. Can't you consider letting him come home now?'

'I'm afraid not,' said Dr Jones. 'Alex is a typical child psychotic in some ways, yet he's very unusual in others. I recognise he suffered profound trauma in the Greek asylum, but his mental history dates back to the age of eight. Currently, Alex is still delusional.

'Firstly, he's pretending to me that he doesn't hear Dr Schultz anymore, but I happen to know he does still hallucinate, because he's admitted hearing Schultz to the nurses. This is most puzzling, and I have to say that Alex is the first case I have ever come across of a patient who hallucinates hearing his psychiatrist. Most puzzling indeed.'

My father kept his mouth shut about the 'special treatment' he had ordered Schultz to perform on me, how he'd ordered him to eradicate timidity, trauma and fear from my personality. Had he been frank and told Dr Jones about this unusual treatment, it might have saved a great deal of time, and me from a lot of heartache to come.

'Secondly,' continued Dr Jones, 'Alex still maintains he killed the little boy, Nikki. No one will ever know the truth about what happened except Alex, but I don't expect he killed him. It's more likely, from what he's reluctantly admitted to Mr Reese, that he couldn't save Nikki, so his mind in denial of this fact has forced him to shoulder all the blame.

'Thirdly, there's Alex's paranoid delusion that someone's been poisoning his food, and that in itself is very serious.'

'But Alex has stopped saying that,' interjected my father.

'Yes, he has,' replied Dr Jones. 'But he's taken to swapping his uneaten meals with the other boys on the ward. Alex doesn't think I know, but the nurses aren't unobservant.'

'Oh!' said my father. 'I didn't realise Alex has been trying to trick us all by lying.'

'It's not exactly lying,' said Dr Jones. 'That would be too harsh a word. Alex is still mentally ill. He's got psychosis. Thus, to a psychotic such as him, the boundaries between truth, twisted truths, and outright lies, has become blurred. Do you understand what I'm saying?'

'Yes, I think so.'

'It's more a matter that Alex, who's now cognitive enough to know there's something still wrong with him, several things in fact, is trying to cover for himself by evasion, denial and lie. It's the impaired coping strategy of a very troubled mentally ill mind.'

'And that's why you say he can't come home yet,' said my father. 'Why I can't bring him back to see you once a week.'

'Yes,' said Dr Jones. 'Any one of these problems would give me cause for concern. All three and it's clear to me that Alex is still a very sick boy.

'This is Alex's second admission to Pen-y-Fal in two years,' he went on. 'What I would hate to see happen is that he becomes more unstable as he gets older, and ends up in a revolving-door pattern of hospital care once he becomes an adult. Now is the time to cut this disordered pattern of behaviour. Now is the time to maintain his treatment until he's cured once and for all.'

'Yes, I see,' said my father. 'I see absolutely. Yes, you must keep Alex at Pen-y-Fal until you're satisfied he's fully recovered.'

After the astonishing events of Tuesday, 12 April, when I was finally forced to recognise that my grandmother was alive and well, life took on afresh aspect for me. There was a bounce in my step, and I was in a happier frame of mind. So happy in fact it even seemed that Schultz was talking to me less. Indeed, over the following weekend I only heard him once when, gazing out of the Day Room window, he suddenly burst into my mind: 'Look out, Alex!' Though you may gaze at the view, they'll never let you go. They're going to keep you here forever, just like Mark!'

I started, as always, to hear Schultz unbidden. And always to taunt unpleasant things, nothing ever encouraging or pleasing. A month ago, even a week ago, I'd have got upset. This weekend, knowing my grandmother was alive and well, I tried to let Schultz's sly words wash over me and drift away. Schultz, I now knew, had been telling me lies for months. Since November I'd had his voice telling me I'd killed my grandmother. That was now blatantly untrue, and I can still recall thinking: Well, if that was untrue, what else has been lies?

I knew I was held at Pen-y-Fal – sectioned – which meant the staff were entitled to lock the doors to keep me on the ward. Indeed, as a detained patient if I ran away the police would catch me and bring me back, and there was nothing anyone could do to stop them.

Yes, I thought, mulling over Schultz's words, they'll never let me go.

And with those maudlin thoughts I felt tears welling up in my eyes and a lump in my throat.

I'd really had enough of my crying turns by now. I felt all cried out and I just didn't want to do it anymore. I was also sure the nurses were pretty fed up with my tears by now. I held my face firm, and stared out of the window.

If I stayed still, I told myself, perhaps no one will notice.

Two tears erupted from my eyes and ran down my face and, unthinking, I raised my hand to wipe them away.

'Are you okay, Alex?' Nurse Clark asked, suddenly at my shoulder.

'Yes, I'll be okay,' I gulped, and remained staring at the view.

'Okay, she said. 'But I'm here if you need me.'

I nodded my head, and watched her reflection in the glass as she walked away.

Two more tears ran free and I felt really upset. Was Dr Jones really going to keep me here for months, or even years?

'Alex, are you okay?' another voice asked.

'Oh, what's the point,' I muttered, giving in and pulling a tissue from my pocket to wipe my eyes.

I turned around and gave Mark a half smile.

'Are you okay?' Mark asked again, a gentle hand on my shoulder.

I squirmed away.

'Only Schultz's voice in my poor head again,' I said.

'Well, try not to think of him,' replied Mark. 'Tell him to go away, and come and play dominoes with me.'

'Yes,' I said with a smile. 'Let's play dominoes and forget all those annoying voices, here or not.'

Mark laughed, and grabbed the box of dominoes off the shelf. I laughed too, my tears of woe to be forgotten for an hour.

As we sat playing dominoes, I found myself pondering my relationship with Mark. He sat blond and beaming opposite me, my only long-term friend on the ward, yet I found myself giving him sly glances as he put domino after domino down, eager to win our game. Mark had always seemed to me a gentle giant, although he wasn't that big really, just bigger than me. I just didn't seem to age or grow, and it was most frustrating to me at that time of my life. It was an annoying fact of life that because I looked ten-years-old, I generally got *treated* by everyone as if I was ten, regardless of the fact I was by now thirteen. Mark was my friend, but I had to recognise he was also unstable and had the potential for terrifying violence. 'Be careful,' Judy had once warned me, 'and don't tell Mark much about yourself.' Well, I reckoned Mark probably now knew more about me than even my father. In my long months of incarceration I had soon run out of conversation, and despite my best efforts to remain circumspect and private I found I just couldn't keep my mouth shut. I'd talked and talked, about everything, from my parents to my home, my time in the Greek asylum, my friends, the 'voices' in my head, my hopes and fears. I just hadn't kept my mouth shut and now it was too late.

I was now in the uncomfortable position that Mark knew too much about me, and in a distracted moment I'd said I loved him. In reality I'd meant not just him but everyone, having discovered my grandmother was alive and well. Mark had totally misunderstood, and being a very lonely boy whose father only visited him a couple of times a year, his mother and sister not once in three years, he'd latched onto my declaration of love like a drowning man to a piece of driftwood. Mark was desperate for love and affection, and now believed it would come from me. I just didn't know how to tell him I didn't want to give it. I would remain Mark's friend forever, for I'm nothing if not loyal, but having uttered the word 'love' I knew it would be the cruellest thing in the world to take back that glimmer of hope.

'Aha!' declared Mark, slamming both hands flat on the table. 'I win.'

I looked down and saw I still had four dominoes left. My attention had not been on the game at all.

'Can we have another game?' Mark asked, his voice almost pleading.

'Why not,' I said. 'Let's have another game, and the loser has to ask Nurse Johnson for a hot chocolate for the winner.'

'You're on,' said Mark, flipping all the dominoes over and swirling them about.

I sat back in my chair and watched Mark, and wondered...

There are many elements that can link to bring about a catastrophe. Now, as I write this tale over forty years later, I can see the synchronicity to this catastrophe started in the third week of April 1977, and it would all be my fault. The first act of this catastrophe had been the way I told Mark about my life. It had been a dangerous thing indeed to pass on such private details to someone diagnosed as a sociopath; dangerous for me, and dangerous for Mark. Once I had spilled out these details, memorised and catalogued by Mark, date by date, fact by fact, I could not take them back, and Mark was too tempted to use them to get what he wanted. He just couldn't see it was wrong to blackmail his closest friend to get what he wanted, and the ramifications would not only devastate me, but ultimately him too.

The countdown to catastrophe really started on Tuesday, 19 April. On Tuesdays Dr Jones conducted ward-round, in which he'd talk to every patient on the ward. Ward-round was from ten till noon, and I knew I'd have a ten-minute session with Dr Jones in which he'd ask me questions, and adjust my medication if need be.

On that Tuesday morning, at 11:00 a.m., I was sat next to Mark trying to fathom out an algebra question set by Mrs Howell.

Mark slyly turned his sheet of paper so I could see the solution, and he flashed me a conspiratorial grin.

'Alex!' called Nurse Clark, 'Doctor will see you now.'

Dr Jones was sat in the Ward Office off the main corridor, Nurse Johnson at his side to take notes.

He asked me the usual range of questions: How are you feeling today? Are you still tearful and unhappy? Do you recognise you've been ill and fantasising? Is Dr Schultz still talking to you?

My answer to every question that day was generally the lie 'no,' for I wanted to be discharged by now. I asked Dr Jones how soon I could go home. After all, I remarked, I knew my grandmother was alive and well now, and I wasn't hearing Dr Schultz either I lied.

'Well,' said Dr Jones, 'you're making progress, so I think I can say you can leave here in weeks rather than months.'

'Two weeks, *three* weeks?' I asked.

'Something a little longer than that, Alex, but we're not talking many months. Perhaps something like six weeks or a little more, but I'll have to see how you do. In the end it's up to you. You're the one who has to make progress and convince me you've recovered.'

And with that my consultation ended, and Dr Jones directed Nurse Clark to take me back to the Day Room.

'Christopher!' Nurse Clark called in the Day Room, and an unhappy fourteen-year-old I didn't know very well got up and followed Nurse Clark out into the corridor.

'Well?' asked Mark, as soon as I sat. 'What's the news?'

'Doctor thinks I can go home in a few weeks... maybe,' I replied.

Mark digested this for a long moment. Then he turned his work around so I couldn't copy his answers.

'You can't go so soon,' Mark said. 'You promised to stay with me. You've still got problems, and you're not well enough to go home.'

'Well, I think that's up to Dr Jones,' I replied. 'He's the boss here. If he says I can go, I'm off.'

'You can't, you mustn't,' retorted Mark in a furious whisper. 'I'll tell him the truth about you. You still hear Schultz. You still think your meals are poisoned, and I'm eating them for you. You still think you killed that kid in Greece. I'm going to tell Jones everything!'

By the end of Mark's tirade I was petrified.

He has the ability to keep me here, I thought. Oh, God, he can really do it!

'Mark!' called Nurse Clark. 'Your turn to see doctor.'

Mark got up from his seat and began to walk away, set off on his mission to tell all about me to Dr Jones.

'Mark, stop!' I shouted.

I threw a textbook as hard as I could, and hit him square between the shoulder blades. Mark cried out in stunned shock and turned to face me. He ducked as I threw another book, swiftly followed by a mug of pencils off the table.

'Alex!' shouted Mr Thomas. 'Stop this at once!'

I took no notice. I flung my chair away and it clattered across the floor, swiftly followed by Mark's chair too. Mr Thomas ran towards me, but I evaded his grasp to run to the far end of the Day Room, upending and throwing anything that came to hand. Eventually cornered and with nowhere else to go, Mr Thomas wrestled me to the floor and held both my arms behind me in an arm-lock. I screamed and shouted, but by now Dr Jones had entered the Day Room to find out what the commotion was. I continued to scream and sob, and the next thing I knew Nurse Clark had pulled my trousers midway down my legs, and Dr Jones gave me an injection in one thigh. Mr Thomas continued to hold my arms, and Nurse Clark sat on my legs until I calmed down.

Once the sedative took effect, Mr Thomas and Nurse Clark manhandled me up off the floor, out of the Day Room, and down to corridor to time-out.

Here I was stripped and a white cotton gown pulled on me. I screamed and shouted at them to leave me alone. Dr Jones now appeared and, whilst the two nurses held me, gave me a second injection in the arm.

Mr Thomas and Nurse Clark sat me on the floor, and all three adults left closing the door behind them.

I could feel myself falling, falling a thousand feet. I slumped onto my side, my head to hit the floor an inch from my eyes. And there I stayed, drugged and no trouble to anyone, locked in time-out for the rest of the day.

Grudges did not seem to last long on Ward 3, for the staff had seen enough tantrums over the years for such events to be commonplace. It was part and parcel of life on a mental ward that such events took place occasionally. Once, when I'd been very ill in December, my tantrums had been such a frequent occurrence I'd been kept in time-out for days at a time. On this occasion I was released at 7:00 p.m., given something to eat, then put to bed. By the following morning the event, though recorded in my notes, was forgotten and forgiven, and my life returned to normal.

Such was the normality of such an event on the ward that the following day Nurse Johnson picked ten boys to go for an after-lunch walk through the grounds to sit at the little wooden pavilion, and I was chosen as well as Mark. Thus ten boys were escorted across the huge lawns to the pavilion by Nurse Johnson and Nurse Clark, there to sit and chat, and gaze at the landscaped grounds of Pen-y-Fal.

As I walked with the other boys, Nurse Johnson up front holding the hand of a boy named Tony, Nurse Clark bringing up the rear and chatting to Christopher, I felt a hand rest on my shoulder and Mark fell into step alongside me.

'Hello,' said Mark. 'You're quiet today.'

He acted as if nothing had happened.

'What did you expect,' I retorted. 'You've ended up in time-out as well as me. It's not very nice, is it?'

'No, it's not very nice,' Mark replied. 'I'm sorry. I can see it was my fault. I *am* sorry, Alex. Can we be friends again, please?'

This was a huge thing for Mark to say. In all the months I'd spent in Mark's company I'd never once heard him apologise, never once heard him admit he had been in the wrong. This was a remarkable development, and it needed a generous response. There was no point in being churlish.

'Yes, we can be friends again,' I said. 'But it all depends on what you told Dr Jones about me, doesn't it.'

'Oh,' exclaimed Mark, 'I never told Jones a thing about you. I swear it.' And with that he licked his finger and crossed his heart.

I looked at Mark for a long moment.

'Friends?' I asked.

'Friends,' Mark replied, and he grasped my arm and squeezed it.

I responded with a smile, but squirmed my arm free using the excuse of doing up the zip of my anorak, for despite the April sunshine there was a chill north wind.

By now Mark was beaming and chatting in excitement, but my mind was far away thinking of my Dad as I watched Nurse Johnson put a tender arm around Tony's shoulder as she walked at the head of our column, now nearly at the pavilion.

'Alex!' Mark said, and I was brought back to reality. 'You haven't been listening, have you?'

'I'm sorry. I thought I heard Schultz,' I lied, knowing he would accept that tale.

'Well,' he exclaimed in exasperation, 'I'll ask you again.' He dropped his voice to a murmur. 'I've decided to run away, just for the afternoon. I want to go to Abergavenny, and I want you to come with me.'

'Won't we get into terrible trouble?' I asked. 'Doctor Jones will do his nut, and so will Nurse Johnson.'

'Oh, let them,' retorted Mark. 'I ran away last September for a few hours and, except for an evening spent in time-out, nothing happened. Are you game for a bit of fun? Please say you are.'

'How can we do it?' I asked. 'We'll never get away.'

'Oh, I've figured it all out.' Mark said with a grin. 'I've been plotting this escape for weeks. Johnson and Clark always sit together at the pavilion. Everyone sits facing outward. The pavilion is a hexagon. We gradually make our way to sit on the opposite side to the nurses, and when they're watching the other boys play catch with the ball, we make a run for some nearby trees. Are you game, or are you chicken?'

'I'm no chicken,' I retorted. 'You just tell me what to do and when.'

Mark grinned, happy that we were friends again.

As soon as we arrived at the pavilion Nurse Johnson fussed around everyone, making sure we were all sat, and then she produced a ball for some of the boys to play catch.

Mark pretended to watch, but he began to edge along the seat, and I followed. Soon the solid central core of the pavilion obscured the ball game, and it also obscured Nurses Johnson and Clark. If I couldn't see them, then they couldn't see us.

'We're never going to get away with this,' I whispered to Mark.

'Oh, yes we will,' he replied. 'You wait and see.'

In a few minutes we were on the opposite side of the pavilion and just twenty yards from a copse of trees and some rhododendron bushes.

'Now!' Mark hissed to me, and suddenly we were both running across the grass.

For such a big boy Mark was surprisingly light of foot as he hopped and skipped between twigs and branches, making no noise at all, and I followed him. Soon the pavilion was out of sight, which meant we couldn't be seen either. We'd done it. We'd escaped the strict supervision of Nurse Johnson for a few hours, and we'd escaped Ward 3. Now Mark and I could just be two friends out for the afternoon.

The suburbs of Abergavenny were smart residential as Mark and I walked the pavement alongside the main road into town.

We'd had a spot of luck soon after escaping from the grounds of Pen-y-Fal. We'd only walked a hundred yards when Mark told me to put on a limp, and he flagged down a passing electric milk float.

'Here, mate,' he called to the driver, as brazen as anything, 'my friend's twisted his ankle. Can you give us a lift back into town?'

'Sure,' the driver replied. 'Hop into the cab with me.'

And so it was that the slowest escape in history took place at the sedate speed of ten miles per hour. We hadn't gone a mile before we saw a police-car speeding in the opposite direction, lights flashing, its destination Pen-y-Fal, the reason Mark and I.

'We're going to get into so much trouble,' I whispered to Mark, the enormity of what I'd done hitting me for the first time. The least of my worries was going to be Dr Jones and three or four hours in time-out, my nemesis was going to be my Dad when he found out.

'Shut up!' Mark hissed into my ear.

The police car didn't slow or pause, but sped on its way, ignoring us completely.

The milk float duly dropped us off in the suburbs of Abergavenny, and Mark and I, arm in arm, marched boldly along Monk Street in the direction of the town centre.

'What are we going to do?' I asked. 'We haven't got any money.'

'I don't need money for what I'm going to do!' Mark declared, a sudden harshness in his voice.

I felt a chill in my bones to hear the determination in his voice.

'Oh?' I replied, trying to keep my voice level. 'What are you going to do?'

'I haven't seen my Dad since last year. He didn't come at Christmas and he didn't come at Easter. I reckon he's due a visit from me. I'm going to his garage and confront him just as he's selling a car to someone. Let's see how he likes that! I want him to realise he just can't abandon me in *that* place, and I want him to bring my mother and sister too.' He raised a hand to wipe tears from his face.

Oh dear, I thought, suddenly seeing the enormity of Mark's scheme for the first time. I'd imagined us to run away for a few hours of fun and a wander of the shops, before we gave ourselves up and were taken home to Pen-y-Fal. Now I realised Mark had a grand plan, and Judy's warnings that Mark was also a sociopath echoed in my mind. I began to tremble, and had a knot of fear deep in the pit of my stomach. The adventure had suddenly become deadly serious, and I was very afraid.

Monk Street was the main highway into the centre of Abergavenny, consisting of housing interspersed with shops. I tried to interest Mark in the shops, pausing at each one to gaze in the window at the contents.

'No!' said Mark every time. 'We must get on. You can look in the windows on our way back.'

My plan to distract Mark failed, and we rushed ever onward, walking faster and faster.

A bus passed us, throwing up a fine spray from the wet tarmac, and it began to brake as it neared a sharp corner. It slowed to a crawl and, just as it rounded the corner, stopped at a bus stop.

'Come on!' said Mark, releasing his grip on my arm to run ahead.

I too began to run to catch up, thinking: We haven't got any money. The conductor is just going to chuck us off. What's Mark up to?

However, Mark had no intention of catching the bus. As soon as he reached the corner he ran across the road, then stopped to stand waiting for me between two parked cars. I began to run faster to keep up.

'Come on!' Mark urged in a shout.

I ran into the road, but hadn't gone three paces when someone suddenly shouted 'Alex, stop!'

I instantly halted and glanced behind me. Who's calling? I wondered. With shock I immediately realised it was the 'voice.'

'Alex, look out!' Mark screamed, and he darted out from between the parked cars to give me a mighty shove with both hands on my chest.

Many things now happened simultaneously. I was lifted clean off my feet and sent flying to land in the gutter behind the bus. However, even as I fell, almost in slow motion, I looked into Mark's eyes as he looked into mine, just for a millisecond, and all I could see was fear.

Then there was a sudden flash of white as a speeding van careered into Mark.

He was dragged under the vehicle as it skidded to a halt.

'Mark!' I screamed, scrambling to my feet.

I ran to the front of the van.

The van driver leapt from his cab, just as half a dozen pedestrians and the bus conductor ran with me to help Mark.

Mark was under the front of the van, his sleeve caught in the mounting of a broken fog light. I took hold of Mark's hand, but though still warm it was quite limp.

'Mark!' I screamed. 'Mark!'

The bus conductor took hold of me and forcibly led me away.

'Come with me, sonny,' he said, treating me like the ten-year-old he believed me to be. 'You must let us grown-ups deal with this. We'll look after your friend.'

He handed me to a woman who took hold of my arm.

I flopped to sit on the pavement, my feet in the gutter.

'Mark's dead!' I cried. 'It's my fault. I got Mark killed. He's dead. Oh God, he's dead.'

'We don't know if your friend is dead,' said the woman gently, her hand on my shoulder. 'Now you must stay calm.'

Just at that moment a police car raced up and two policemen leapt from their car to help Mark. One carried a blanket.

I watched them drag Mark by his arm out from under the van.

'It's alright,' the woman kept saying. 'It's going to be alright. The policemen will look after your friend.'

Several of the men now held the blanket between them like a screen to hide Mark as the policemen worked to save his life.

The men began to lower the screen, and I broke free of the woman's grasp to run into the road to see if Mark was okay.

I pushed through the crowd.

Mark was lying flat on his back in the road. He had a wicked gash on his forehead and his face was a mask of blood, his coat was torn and dirty, and he had lost a shoe.

The blanket was handed to the policemen, who laid it across Mark, covering his torso and head.

One of the pedestrians began to recite the *Lord's Prayer*, and everyone dropped their heads in respect.

'Mark!' I screamed. 'Mark!'

I fell to the floor and held him tight.

'Here,' said one of the policemen, 'that will do no good, son. Come away with me and sit in the police car.'

I was sobbing hysterically by now, as the two policemen lifted me off Mark's body as I clung to him.

'What's your name?' one of the policemen asked. 'And where do you live? We'll have to arrange for someone to take you home.'

'My name is Alexander Sinclair,' I replied, 'and I don't have a home. I come from Pen-y-Fal Hospital.'

'Was your friend's name Mark Stevens?' the policeman asked.

'Yes,' I replied. 'Oh, Mark,' I cried. 'Oh, Mark.' I began to cry long drawn out howls.

Another blanket was produced, and the policeman began to wrap it around me, just as another police car arrived, accompanied by an ambulance.

I sat in the back of the police car, sobbing in anguish, just as Schultz began to rant in my head, telling me his insane poison about how everyone I loved would die because of me; I was cursed. I beat my head with my fists, and screamed another long drawn-out howl.

The policeman sat beside me held my arms down to stop me hurting myself.

The other policeman came over, just as a stretcher was produced from the ambulance.

'Here, Richard,' said the policeman holding me. 'These are the two boys who absconded from Pen-y-Fal. I think you'd better get on the radio to call up a car to take this boy back. He's becoming more unstable with every minute. The last thing we need now is a mental child on our hands.'

I watched the ambulance men lift Mark's body off the road and place him on the stretcher.

I screamed, soprano and anguished, broken by deep sobs.

Mark was dead, and now no one, from my father to Dr Jones and Mr Reese could deny it was my fault. I was cursed.

CHAPTER 7

# Consequences

I stood gazing into the shop window at the wonderful display sugared bonbons, bars of chocolate stacked high, long candy canes like small striped walking sticks. For a long moment I felt as if I could almost taste the wonderful confectionary. Then I heard the foot-falls of someone running, and they were getting louder.

'Alex!' shouted a voice. 'Come on.'

I turned from the shop window and began to run, chasing the figure pounding away down the pavement.

'Mark!' I shouted. 'Stop! Oh, please stop!'

As we neared the end of the street my cries to Mark to stop became more panicked. Mark *had* to stop, he *must not* step off the kerb. Mark halted at the far end of the pavement, and then I noticed he only wore one shoe.

'Oh, Mark,' I exclaimed to his back, 'thank you for stopping.'

Mark turned around, as if in slow motion, and it was then I saw his coat was torn, and his face was a mask of blood.

I screamed again and again, just as a passer-by took hold of my shoulders and began to shake me.

I awoke in my room at Pen-y-Fal, and found Judy shaking my shoulders to wake me from my nightmare.

'Are you awake, Alex?' she asked. 'You've been dreaming again, haven't you? Can you tell me about it?'

I stared into Judy's blue eyes that mirrored my blue eyes. I began to cry silently, and tears ran in little rivulets down my face, but I made no sound, no speech.

'Oh, Alex,' Judy said gently, and she sat on the side of my bed to hug me, giving me some comfort in my distress. I knew from experience that she would not let go of me until I calmed down.

Then, to my surprise, Judy too began to weep, the tears running down her face. So there the two of us sat, hugging each other in a mental institution, crying in the middle of the night.

I'm sure, in hindsight, it was not very professional for Judy to sit sobbing, arm in arm with a patient. But she had nursed Mark for nearly three years, and his death left a great void on the ward.

I'd been back at Pen-y-Fal a week, returned by the police after the death of Mark.

The policemen had tried to question me, but I was too traumatised by the event to be of any use. Dr Jones told them I was too ill to be interviewed, and he made them leave. There was one thing every witness had said, each corroborating the other, and that was Mark had safely crossed Monk Street, but he ran back to save me from being hit by the speeding van. Mark had sacrificed himself for me.

On my return Dr Jones had examined me. He checked me over physically to see I was okay. Sadly, I was mentally far from well. I refused to talk, and just stared at the wall, or the door, or the floor, depending on what position Dr Jones put me in. He diagnosed a form of catatonia triggered by deep trauma. When my father hurried from Cardiff to Pen-y-Fal to see me, Dr Jones told him that the condition might just suddenly cease, or it might remain impairing me for a long time. It would just take time for me to heal my mental wounds. That first night Dr Jones gave me an injected sedative, and Nurse Johnson and Judy put me to bed, back in Room 2 all by myself. In my catatonic state I let them put my pyjamas on me and put me to bed, and all this without a word said by me.

I had lain in bed staring at the ceiling, my thoughts of poor Mark. Mark had died to save my life. In the end poor Mark, labelled schizophrenic and sociopath, had paid the ultimate price to save me. I owed him my life, but didn't have the faintest idea how to repay such a huge debt. It was at this point I fell asleep, assisted by Dr Jones's potent drugs. However, I'd only been asleep an hour before the nurses on duty were roused by my screams. I was fortunate that one of the nurses on duty that night had been Judy, and she had a very sympathetic and caring attitude. She came into my room, sat on a chair at the side of my bed holding my hand, and told me comforting things as she endeavoured to put my mind at rest.

For the first week after Mark's death I was terrible to handle. I would not talk. I became aggressive at mealtimes, refusing to eat and ended up in time-out for throwing my food on the floor, and I kept biting my hands until they bled.

All the while this was happening I had the ranting voice of Schultz telling me not to talk. Words were weapons that could be used against me. Look what my slip of the tongue had caused when I told Mark I loved him. Mark had taken my words to heart, and he paid for them with his life. The consequence was I refused to talk. I refused to talk to Dr Jones, I refused to talk to Mr Reese, I refused to talk to Judy, Nurse Johnson and Mr Thomas, or anyone else in fact, and I refused to talk to my Dad. I just went mute, which Dr Jones told my father was a result of the trauma of seeing Mark killed.

'Give him time,' Dr Jones told my father. 'Alex will start to talk again when he wants to communicate with us. When that moment arrives I can begin to treat him. He will recover, I do assure you.'

In the meantime, mute and appearing semi-catatonic, I became frustrated and easily distressed. The consequence, either of self-injury such as beating my head on the wall, or even throwing my food on the floor, was I ended up in time-out more and more often. It was boring in its blandness, just white walls, floor and door to stare at, but it was always warm and quiet, and it wasn't populated by annoying people who wanted to talk to me. In time-out I usually got some tablets to keep me quiet, and then I was left to my own devices, which mainly consisted of sitting on the floor in the corner, pondering my past, my future, and often there was Dr Schultz's 'voice' giving me guidance: 'Be wary of the kindness of the nurses; they have an alternate purpose.' 'Your food has drugs in it to make you talk; be careful.' And on and on.

In the first week of May my father was summoned to a meeting with Dr Jones. The meeting started off cordially as the psychiatrist explained to him that I was a very traumatised and sick boy. Dr Jones said they had tried all the normal avenues open to them – drugs and psychoanalysis – all to no avail. It was as if there was a wall in my mind, and Dr Jones and Mr Reese couldn't find a way around it. The fact I was presently suffering hysterical catatonia was unhelpful, so Dr Jones was now looking for alternate methods of treatment. It was at this point that the conversation took a decidedly uncomfortable turn, as my father told me many years later.

Dr Jones told my father he'd telephoned Dr Schultz in West Germany to ask him for some information about how he had treated me after my rescue from the Greek asylum. Dr Schultz had been evasive, said Dr Jones, until he told him what had happened and that I was currently presenting as catatonic. Dr Jones told my father that Schultz admitted to using Sodium Pentothal on me after my rescue from the Attica, and had 'built a wall' in my mind between me and my traumatic memories.

In the late 1940s Sodium Pentothal had been used in Germany on holocaust survivors to make them more receptive to treatment for their traumatic ordeals. Sodium Pentothal was misguidedly known as a 'truth drug' in the 1970s, mainly because of its use by the security services in the interrogation of captured enemy agents in the Cold War. In reality Sodium Pentothal is a powerful anaesthetic. When used in a small dosage in psychiatric treatment it weakens the brain's resistance and the patient becomes more receptive to talking about the past and to suggested ideas and treatment. However, its use was very controversial.

Dr Jones demanded to know from my father precisely what had been done to me. Schultz's 'treatment' had brought me back to seeming normality on the surface, but Dr Jones was far more interested to know what had been the drawbacks of my treatment. What was hidden beneath the surface? The treatment had clearly now failed and left me a mental wreck.

My father reluctantly told Dr Jones that Dr Edgar Schultz was West Germany's leading expert on mind control. He was a prominent psychiatrist in his own right, but I had been so dreadfully mentally damaged by the time my father rescued me from Greece that there wasn't much left to work with. I'd been mentally destroyed. My father told Jones that he had been a Liaison Officer to the Bundesnachrichtendienst (West German Intelligence). He had, with their help, taken it upon himself to pay for me to be treated by the top man – Dr Schultz – the BND used to treat traumatised personnel rescued from behind the Iron Curtain. Schultz had convinced my father that what would work on an adult could be applied to a child. My father had therefore told Dr Schultz to use whatever treatment he felt necessary to restore me to health. Finally, my father admitted to Dr Jones, he had ordered Schultz to use his special skills, whilst he was treating me, to eradicate fear and timidity from my personality. Evidently Dr Schultz's treatment had not worked in the desired way. Timidity and fear were now powerful facets of my personality.

My father said he had received back a son outwardly restored to health, with an apparently well-adjusted personality. But the truth was, he now realised, I had experienced such profound trauma in the Attica, seen such dark things, that I was a mental wreck beneath the surface. Clearly a lot of damage had been done. He was forced to admit that Dr Schultz's treatment had been a catastrophe.

My father subsided into silence and sat awaiting Dr Jones's verdict.

My father later recalled that Dr Jones just sat twiddling his pen.

'Can Alex be restored to health?' my father eventually asked.

Dr Jones made it clear he thought it had been the utmost folly to let Dr Schultz practice 'adult psychiatric treatments on a child' and to try to alter my personality. However, he respected the fact that my father had rescued from Greece a mentally devastated child, and so he had acted with the best of intentions. He went further and said he now understood my current breakdown, which had started last November, was a sign I'd never really recovered. It was now clear to Dr Jones that Schultz's treatment, especially the use of Sodium Pentothal, was the root cause of my inability to cope with the realities of life. Whenever a traumatic event occurred, such as the fictitious death of my grandmother, and now the real death of Mark, my mind retreated behind the potent treatment – the 'programming' – of Dr Schultz, and I collapsed a complete mental wreck unable to handle reality.

'Alex was only eleven-years-old when Dr Schultz practiced this treatment on him,' explained Dr Jones. 'His mind was too young to cope with the powerful orders and counter-orders Schultz put into him. He is now a child with a mind in turmoil. I believe Alex is once again hearing Schultz's 'voice,' and he is listening to his orders and counter-orders.'

'But surely you can undo the damage Dr Schultz has done,' my father said.

'Listen,' said Dr Jones. 'Schultz used Sodium Pentothal on Alex. That is the most powerful drug there is to place suggestions into a person's mind. It had dramatic effects on adults. Used on a child, God knows what has happened. I don't know what else Schultz did to Alex, and I don't know how much damage has been done. I can't go off willy-nilly practicing outlandish treatments on him, and anyway I would refuse to do so on ethical grounds."

'Please, Doctor,' said my father, 'do what you can for my son.'

'I don't know where to begin to heal the damage. Psychiatrically and psychologically, Alex is a real mess. The way Mark died would be traumatic enough for any normal child, but Alex is delusional and psychotic. And mixed into all this, somewhere, is the 'treatment' of Dr Schultz. I don't know, Mr Sinclair, I really don't. I will do what I can. But that is all I can promise you. Alex is a likeable boy. I would hate to see him end up a long-term patient, lasting into adulthood.'

Life back on the ward was an unpleasant experience for me. Mark had been such a buoyant personality his death left a great void on the ward. He'd often been noisy and the cause of mischief, but I missed him terribly. Mark had been the oldest boy on the ward, now most of the boys were my age. They were all mentally ill anyway, but they wanted to chat and play all the time. Everyone, that is, except Christopher. Christopher was a dour boy, always keen to play Scrabble, but he had tried to poison – to kill – his sister for blabbing in school that he was a bed-wetter. The consequence was he'd been sectioned and sent to Pen-y-Fal.

Every day the nurses made me get dressed and go to the Day Room, and I hated it. I hated the familiarity of the boys who wanted to talk, but didn't understand when I refused to respond. 'Stuck-up' or 'Snob' were the taunts I now received. The trouble was the boys were not the only voices I could hear. I had Schultz talking in my head, telling me things such as: 'You are in danger; everyone is the enemy!' or 'Don't trust the nurses, they're poisoning your food with drugs to make you talk!' This state of affairs lasted a fortnight.

On the fourteenth day, as I was sat watching television in the Day Room one afternoon, Nurse Clark tapped me on the shoulder, and said: 'Alex, you've got a visitor.'

I looked questioningly at her, and it must have been obvious from my expression that I was puzzled. This was a Tuesday, and therefore not a day when my Dad was due to visit.

'It's okay,' she said with a smile. 'Your visitor is your Auntie Eileen.'

Now I was really astonished. Auntie Eileen was my Dad's sister-in-law, and I hadn't seen her in over a year. A little nagging worry began in my mind, and I was fearful that she'd come to tell me my Dad was ill or something, and would not be visiting me for a while.

I followed Nurse Clark from the ward and down the stairs to the Visiting Room.

At the door, Nurse Clark said: 'I'll return in half an hour. Enjoy your visit.'

And with that she ushered me in and closed the door behind me.

My aunt, dressed in a sheepskin coat, a headscarf over her hair, was stood with her back to me gazing out of the window.

Although she must have heard me enter the room and the door close behind me, she did not turn around, and so I just stood and waited. One minute passed, then two. In the end I felt prompted to cough to attract her attention.

She turned, as if in slow motion, and it was *not* my Auntie Eileen.

My mother, minus her glasses, blinked at me myopically, and said: 'Hello, Alex.'

I stood rooted to the spot, my mind numb with terror.

'Not going to speak?' she asked.

She must have known I'd gone mute, so she shrugged nonchalantly and said: 'It's okay.'

And still I stood, too terrified to move.

She crossed the room until she halted before me.

She was silent for a long moment, her eyes boring into me, into my very soul it seemed. Then she blinked slowly, almost reptilian-like, and the spell was broken.

Although I greatly feared my mother, part of me knew she could do me no harm whilst I was in this place. I believed I was beyond her reach. In a sense I was correct, physically speaking, but it would transpire I was not immune to her touch, metaphorically speaking.

'I've got some bad news,' she said. 'Your father was knocked down by a hit and run driver this morning. He's dead.'

My mind, as fragile as it was, went numb.

Although I could feel tears welling up in my eyes, I was too shocked to react. I just froze, to the extent it seemed to me that even my heart had stopped.

She regarded me for a long moment with that magnetic gaze of hers, much like a snake mesmerises its prey before it strikes.

In the end she said: 'You're here for the moment, but eventually you'll have to come back to me. No one wants you, and neither do I. When all this nonsense is over,' and she waved an arm airily about the room, 'you *will* come back to me, and then things will happen my way.'

She was silent again for a moment, then said: 'As soon as you come back, I'm returning you to the Attica.' She nodded her head firmly. 'Oh, yes,' she continued, 'that's what's going to happen. Everyone knows you're mad, and as your mother I have the right to do exactly what I want with you.'

She rummaged with one hand in her handbag, a smile on her face. It wasn't a normal smile. It was a grimace. When she smiled like that I knew she was capable of great evil. She withdrew her closed hand from her bag, and held it to me.

'Here, I've brought something of your father's for you,' she said. 'A memento.'

I held out my hand.

She placed the small object in my palm, and then gently closed my fingers around it.

'It's time for me to go now, Alex,' she said brightly. She paused for a moment, then added: 'I think you know what to do with this.'

She let go of my hand and turned abruptly, making me jump. She went to the door and stopped, but did not turn to face me.

'Goodbye, Alex,' she said, still looking away.

Then she opened the door, stepped out and closed it quietly behind her.

I looked down at my hand and slowly opened my fingers.

The object was my father's small pearl-handled penknife. The one he used to open mail and occasionally clean his pipe.

I stood silently regarding it for nearly five minutes.

My father was dead. Now there was no hope for me; no one who would protect me anymore. And once I got out of this place my mother was going to take me back to the Greek asylum. I was in a Catch 22. Either stay mad and locked away in Pen-y-Fal for the rest of my days, or be returned to the Attica. There was no way out. Only now I had a way out. My mother had given me my father's penknife, and as good as told me what to do with it. As I stood for those five minutes I decided what I must do.

I placed the penknife in my pocket, and then just stood gazing blankly at the wall.

My mind was beginning to shut down and I was entering another place. Everything seemed distant to me. No more pain, no more anguish, no more self-hate. Only oblivion. It was becoming a very attractive prospect.

On Nurse Clark's return she was surprised to find me alone, stood staring blankly across the room. Her surprise was that my so-called aunt had left. As to my mental state, it was nothing unusual. The nurses were used by now to my various moods, and as to my blank stare she obviously thought it was my catatonia and nothing to be remarked upon. She was not to know, of course, that hidden behind my blank eyes I was mentally entering an end game.

Oh, not to think anymore, I thought. How wonderful.

On my return to the ward, I walked calmly down the corridor, entered my room and quietly closed the door behind me.

The only thing that was in my mind was that my father was dead, gone forever. I wanted to join him wherever he had gone. How wonderful the notion of oblivion seemed to me at that moment. And now I had my Dad's penknife, and therefore the means to do it. Indeed, my mother had even suggested what I should do with it.

I took the little penknife from my pocket and sat upon my bed.

I opened out the blade and stared at it for what seemed like an eternity, but could only have been a few minutes. My mind had lost the comprehension of time.

So there's an end to it all, I thought. It is the end of the world.

I held the knife tight in one hand, forced the sharp tip hard into my right wrist and, with a sudden slash, cut my wrist. I then cut my left wrist. I soon realised I had not made a very good job of my suicide attempt, for despite the copious amount of blood I shed over my clothes, bedding and floor, I was sure it wasn't enough to kill me. I would have to do something else.

I raised the knife to the side of my neck, where I assumed my jugular to be.

Just at that moment, with my hand poised to strike and blood everywhere, Nurse Johnson entered my room to find out why I wasn't in the Day Room.

With one look, at the blood all over my jumper, trousers and bed, my hand and knife at my neck, she flew across the room and wrestled the knife from my hand.

'Help me! Help me!' she began shouting.

Nurse Clark appeared in the doorway, and one glance sent her in panicked flight.

I heard the sound of the ward alarm ringing, and within seconds Nurse Clark was back with Mr Thomas.

I was quite hysterical by now, sobbing and thrashing about on the bed as Nurse Johnson and Mr Thomas held me, each with a hand grasped firmly about a bleeding wrist.

Dr Jones now appeared, and injected me with a sedative. He then dressed my wounds with butterfly stitches and bandages.

I was then put to bed, with Nurse Johnson sat on a chair at my side, and still I had said not a word.

A nurse sat in my room all night, and at eight the following morning she was replaced by Judy.

She said a few words to me, but I really wasn't listening.

I lay against my pillow propped up against the headboard, and stared at the wall opposite.

The accumulated trauma of Mark's death, news of my father's death, my suicide attempt, had left my mind cold and isolated. I was hardly aware of my environment.

About mid-morning I heard the door open, and then a man in a sports jacket sat on the edge of my bed.

'Hello, Alex,' said my father.

I began to scream, and it was high-pitched and without end.

The only person I seemed to bond with was Judy, so she was now made responsible for me. She was taken off the duty roster, so that she came on duty at 8:00 a.m. and stayed on duty – and with me full time – until 6:00 p.m. For a long time after my suicide attempt I was kept locked in my room. Every item, from my mug of tea, glass of water, to knives and forks, were logged in and out of my room, and I was supervised the entire time I had them. I would not be given the opportunity of smashing a mug or glass to cut myself, and neither was I permitted to have possession of a knife or fork unless it was to eat my meal. And all the time I had a nurse – Judy – shadowing me; watching me in my room, even following me to the toilet.

Despite my silence and semi-catatonia, my mind functioned. Everyone, especially my father, had been puzzled how I'd managed to get hold of his penknife. He even suggested that perhaps he'd dropped it, and I had craftily picked it up. I was not inclined to tell anyone my mother had given it to me, and why. I felt really stupid and angry with myself that my mother had almost succeeded in tricking me into killing myself. A telephone call to my Auntie Eileen revealed she had not visited me at all, and everyone was puzzled to know who this strange woman had been. I was determined not to make matters worse, yet, by telling that it had been my Mum. My situation was bad enough as it was, without that added complication. If and when I got better, there would be plenty of time to tell my father.

Because I was restricted to my room, Judy was made responsible for my exercise, and so every morning I'd put on my coat and shoes, and Judy and Mr Thomas would take me downstairs and out into the car park. There, with both nurses firmly holding my hands, they took me for a brisk walk to the pavilion and back.

All the time I was in Judy's company she talked and talked, telling me what a nice day it was, how I was looking much better, how I should try to put the past behind me, what a nice meal lunch was today. At the end of every sentence she would conclude with a question: 'Are you feeling better today?' 'Did you enjoy your walk?' 'Did you enjoy lunch?' Sadly I never responded, for I had Schultz's warnings echoing in my mind that anything I said could be used as a weapon against me. The result was I stayed mute. I'd smile and nod, or sometimes I'd spontaneously start to cry, but that was about as responsive I'd be. Eventually I could tell even Judy was becoming short of temper that I wouldn't respond. She knew full well I had the ability to talk and could, on occasion, be quite an eloquent child. I was just being difficult, but then who could blame me for having witnessed – having caused – Mark's death.

I suppose, in hindsight, I was presenting as very mentally ill, but it just didn't seem that way to me at the time. I was in a nice cosy environment on the ward, albeit locked in my room all the time, except for an hour every afternoon when I was escorted to the Day Room to watch the television. I had my meals brought to me, and I had Judy with me all day, always with a smile upon her face and totally without malice towards me. She was caring and soft of voice, ever ready to give me a hug if I needed it.

Despite the way I settled into a quiet, if institutional, way of life on Ward 3, it was no good for me. I was becoming too settled and, said Dr Jones to my father one day in May, I was making no effort to recover. Dr Jones was very concerned, for despite the regular times I met Mr Reese every other afternoon, I wasn't making the slightest effort to meet him even halfway. Mr Reese would ask me how I felt, and did I feel any better? I'd sit on the chair before him and was completely distracted, gazing around the room, often humming Nikki's tune to myself, my self-created wall of isolation away from people.

'This is no good,' Dr Jones told my father. 'We're losing Alex, and I don't know how to bring him back. I'd welcome any suggestions you can make. Can you telephone Dr Schultz for his advice? I'm convinced his treatment is the root cause of Alex's problems. Dr Schultz used very unconventional methods to treat him. The only way I'm going to get through to him is to undermine Schultz's treatment and by-pass what he installed in young Alex's mind.'

'I will telephone Dr Schultz this evening,' my father said. 'There must be something we can do. Alex has been locked-in for weeks now, and I really don't know what's going to become of him unless you can bring him back to a normal mental state.'

'Regrettably I can answer that question,' said Dr Jones. 'Unless I can bring Alex back, he will become a long-term patient on Ward 3, just like Mark was, albeit for different reasons, and when he reaches maturity, he'll be transferred to the main hospital here at Pen-y-Fal. I would hate to see that fate befall him.'

'Rest assured, Dr Jones,' replied my father. 'I will telephone Dr Schultz this evening, and I will come back with an answer.'

And so on the evening of Thursday, 12 May, my father telephoned Dr Schultz in Westphalia, West Germany, to ask for help.

My father explained to Dr Schultz that I was a child who had become borderline catatonic, and that my cure of 1974 had completely failed. I had refused to talk since the death of my friend, I refused to respond to Dr Jones, and I'd tried to commit suicide. Dr Jones had expressed deep concern that I'd been treated with Sodium Pentothal after my rescue from the Attica. Obviously the treatment had worked, almost. However, I was now in such a disordered state of mind that Dr Jones was beginning to consider the possibility that I might never be mentally well again.

Dr Schultz listened to everything my father had to say, and five years later my father told me what Dr Schultz had said.

Dr Schultz explained to my father that I was so mentally damaged after my rescue from Greece that I had been very challenging to treat. To start with nothing had worked, and he'd had to contend with my screaming fits day and night. It was only then, very reluctantly, that he'd decided to use Sodium Pentothal as a way of making me talk about the past and make me susceptible to suggested thought patterns that were altogether healthier. When Dr Schultz treated traumatised adults he often, under drug treatment, gave them a key-word that would allow him back into their subconscious with minimal drug intervention. Thus, explained Dr Schultz, to one patient the key-word was *Mondlicht* (moonlight), to another *Liegestuhl* (deckchair). These key-words were crucial to the patient, for if known by a third party they could be used to detrimental effect.

'Did you give Alex a key-word?' asked my father.

'Yes,' replied Schultz, 'but if I tell it to you, you must only ever use it on this one occasion to bypass his catatonia. It must never be used to force Alex to obey a command, such as "clean your room." To do so would be catastrophic.'

'Yes, I understand,' my father replied. 'I will not tell the key-word to Dr Jones, and I will only use it once to break through Alex's catatonic barrier.'

'Good,' said Dr Schultz. 'Alex's key-word is *Blumenchen* (little flower), as part of the Wandervögel poem: *Blumenchen, Blumenchen, komm mit mir. Furchtet euch nicht for der Darkelheit. Blumenchen, Blumenchen, komm im der Licht mit mir* – Little flower, little flower, come with me. Don't be afraid of the darkness. Little flower, little flower, come into the light with me.'

'If I use the key-word and poem,' said my father, 'what should I expect as a reaction?'

'Well, to start with Alex may become very upset, as he mourns the loss of his friend, and by this I mean the child killed in the road accident. It should not affect his continuing PTSD over the death of the child in Greece. Once you have used this word to get through to Alex, hand him over for treatment by Dr Jones. He seems very competent practitioner to me, and I can think of no one better to defuse his trauma over the loss of his friend, or to treat him for his psychosis.'

And with that the conversation concluded with my father thanking Dr Schultz, and Dr Schultz asking my father to let him know what happened to me when I got better.

Friday, 13 May, was the fateful day to confront me at Pen-y-Fal, and during the journey he rehearsed how he was going to handle the situation. He drove the fifty miles from Cardiff to the hospital. My father was no psychiatrist, and all this talk of drugs, PTSD, key-words and poems had him largely baffled. All he knew was that he wanted me back to normality, whatever the price.

As it would transpire, actually, my Dad would ultimately prove to be my salvation. The trouble was no one knew it yet.

Arriving at Pen-y-Fal, my father met with Dr Jones and explained what Dr Schultz had told him, but he would not tell him the key-word or poem. Dr Jones was aghast, with all this talk of mental acrobatics, Sodium Pentothal, and now a mysterious key-word and poem. He had never heard of such practices, even at seminars, and he told my father he thought the whole gambit of tools Dr Schultz had used on me sounded like they came from the Dark Ages of psychiatric medicine. He was not at all keen to see such practices used on his ward.

'Please,' pleaded my father. 'Let me have twenty minutes alone with Alex. He's catatonic and psychotic. He's difficult and aggressive. He's tried to commit suicide. He refuses to talk. In short he's a psychiatric mess. What harm can I do? He can hardly get any worse.'

Dr Jones mulled my father's words over for what seemed like an eternity until finally he nodded his head.

'Okay,' he said. 'You can have twenty minutes with your son. I owe you that much grace, but I'm not at all happy about this.'

I clearly remember that day. Judy was sat on a chair with a magazine. I had a *Tintin* book opened on my bed, but was presently stood staring blankly out of the window. The moment Dr Jones entered my room I knew something was up, for my father followed him into my room. We normally met in the Visiting Room.

My father smiled at me and, although I wasn't good at reading faces, I thought he looked tense.

Dr Jones exchanged a few words with Judy, and then they both left, closing the door behind them.

My father sat on my bed.

'Alex,' he said, 'come and sit with me. I want to talk to you.'

I sat next to my father on the bed, and stared at my feet.

'Alex,' said my father, 'will you talk to me? Will you tell me how you're feeling today? Is there anything I can do for you?'

I continued to stare at my feet, but slowly shook my head. I could feel tears welling up behind my eyes, but I so much didn't want to cry in front of my father.

'Alex,' my father said more firmly, the softness fading from his voice. 'Please talk to me. You must talk, or you're going to have to stay here. Do you want that to happen?'

I shook my head again, but now there could be no hiding my tears. They ran down my nose as I continued to stare at my feet.

'Alex!' said my father, his voice firm and commanding. 'Stop this. Talk to me now!'

I stifled a sob, the noise emanating from me sounding like a snort. Now I was crying openly.

'Okay, Alex,' my father said, his voice soft once more. 'I had a long talk about you with Dr Schultz last night.'

That got my attention; broke through my mental barrier. I looked up at my father and wiped the tears from my face with one hand.

'We had a very long talk,' continued my father, 'and he has a message for you. It's a message from me too, and once I give you the message, Dr Schultz says you must not refuse to talk anymore. The message is "*Blumenchen*."'

Then he recited the poem.

It is a very strange thing to describe, all these years later, but it felt like someone had put a knitting-needle into my ear and swirled my brain about. I had, simultaneously, the most dreadful flashbacks to my time in Greece, the death of Nikki, my time with Dr Schultz, my mother's attempt to murder me, the death of Mark, and my suicide attempt.

I fell into my father's arms sobbing deeply, traumatised beyond words.

My father held me tight, and talked softly to me, promising me that I would get better, and then we'd have a wonderful life together. Finally, my father asked – commanded – me to speak.

'Oh, I'm s... so s... sad, Dad,' I stammered. 'Mark died because of me. How can I live with that? Seeing Nikki die was terrible. Seeing Mark k... killed was worse. The van smashed him in the street, and now he's dead and gone. He died to save me.'

I was broken by deep sobs as my father held me, and could feel myself trembling and shaking all over.

'Now look, Alex,' my father said, keen to reinforce Schultz unusual treatment. 'I want you to get better. You've been here for nearly six months. This is no good. You've got to talk to Dr Jones. Remember Dr Schultz's secret word to you: *Blumenchen*. If he was here he'd order you to help Dr Jones to make you get better. Will you do that for me? Will you make an effort to get better?'

'Y... yes, Dad,' I said. 'I'll try. But I miss Nikki and Mark so much. I miss them, Dad, I miss them. They both died because of me.' And with that I broke into deep sobs again.

My father sat holding me for nearly twenty minutes.

When he was sure I'd composed myself, he got up and went to my door. He went out, closing the door behind him, and I was left alone for nearly fifteen minutes.

When the door eventually opened, Judy came in with a cautious smile upon her face.

'Alex,' she said gently, 'are you okay?'

'Yes,' I said. I got up from my bed and ran into her arms, adding: 'I w... want to get better now.'

# CHAPTER 8

# Reconciliation

I t was a bright sunny afternoon on the ward, and I was sat with Christopher in the Day Room watching a film on the television when a boy named Kevin came and sat with us.

'Hi,' said Kevin. 'What's the film?'

'*The Hound of the Baskervilles*,' replied Christopher. 'But it's a secret. Mr Thomas thinks we're watching the tennis.'

'Oh,' said Kevin, 'why's it a secret?'

'Shhh,' I interrupted. 'Mr Thomas said it's too dramatic, a s... sort of horror film. We're not supposed to be watching it.'

'Ooo,' said Kevin. 'Can I watch too?'

'Yes,' hissed Christopher. 'Now shut up. We're coming to the exciting bit.'

Kevin sat down and watched in fascinated horror as Sir Henry Baskerville was chased across the sinister moors at night by a huge hound, a monstrous beast that glowed in the dark. Sherlock Holmes, played by Basil Rathbone, was in closing fast, and the film was just about to reach its climax when... Mr Thomas stepped before us and changed the channel on the television.

'Oh,' complained Christopher, 'we were just getting to the good bit.'

'I told you boys not to watch that film,' said Mr Thomas. 'Now, if you're not content to watch the tennis I'll turn the television off.'

Christopher stormed off down the Day Room to stare moodily out of a window. Kevin and I agreed to sit watching the tennis, but we'd have much rather seen the end of the film.

Kevin Upton was a red-haired boy of my age, and we'd become good friends. Kevin had the bed next to mine, now that I'd been moved back from Room 2 to one of the six-bed dormitories again. He'd had been sent to Pen-y-Fal because he had a psychotic illness, which meant he was often delusional and suffered hallucinations.

Both Kevin and I suffered a similar illness. In my case, by now late May, it was largely under control. In Kevin's case he still had a long journey ahead of him, and told me Dr Jones was trying different medications on him to see which worked best. When he was lucid, Kevin was great fun to be with: funny, witty and intelligent.

On his bad days he behaved like he was insane, huddled on the floor in the corner of the Day Room, sobbing at the horrible hallucinations out to get him. The consequence was Kevin often ended up in time-out.

Well, it was a bad idea for Kevin to have sat with Christopher and me to watch *The Hound of the Baskervilles.* All was quiet until after tea that day, then Kevin left the Day Room to go to the toilet. Suddenly the peace and tranquillity of the ward was shattered by a terrified scream out in the corridor, and Kevin ran back in.

'It's the hound!' he screamed, slamming the double doors behind him. 'The hound is out there waiting for me. Oh, please, won't someone help me?'

Nurse Johnson and Mr Thomas hurriedly took a sobbing Kevin out of the Day Room, his fate a sedative to calm him down and an hour in time-out.

I felt great compassion for Kevin because I knew what he must be going through. When I had suffered my first psychotic illness at the age of nine, I had become delusional and terrified that there were aliens – Daleks – in my house waiting to get me. Now, a month short of my fourteenth birthday, I still suffered hallucinations, but they were generally auditory, i.e. Dr Schultz talking to me, and occasionally tactile, i.e. I believed – and could feel – someone grabbing my hands.

To lose control of one's mind in such a way can be terrifying, for one loses the ability to tell reality from fiction. It's rather like dreaming whilst you're awake, and one soon loses one's grip on reality.

Regardless of Dr Jones's treatment of me for psychosis, Mr Reese was also endeavouring to treat my Post Traumatic Stress Disorder. I was obsessive that I'd killed Nikki in Greece, and that I had now killed Mark as well. I would not listen to all Mr Reese's arguments that I was not to blame. It was all well and good for Mr Reese. He hadn't seen Nikki die; he hadn't been left locked up with his dead body for over twenty-four hours. Indeed, Dr Jones and Mr Reese were not responsible for Mark's death either. That was my fault, and I wouldn't listen to all their placatory words as they tried to persuade me I was not to blame. The trouble was I knew I *was. I* had been at fault. *I* had seen Mark killed. *I* had seen his smashed body afterwards. I would challenge anyone, even an adult, to go through such terrible events and emerge unscathed in some way. The trouble was when Nikki died I was a mere ten-years-old. When I got Mark killed I was just thirteen. Such events would mark anyone for life, and my mental scars ran very deep indeed. So deep, in fact, that I refuse to accept Mr Reese's placatory words.

'You must not blame yourself.' Mr Reese said to me at every meeting. 'You must try to be kind to yourself.'

However, I did blame myself, and I would not be kind to myself.

As May progressed it became clear that I was becoming more and more settled on the ward. At the start of my illness the previous November I had often become frantic and hysterical, screaming to my father to take me home. Indeed, even in March I still made my father's visits a misery as he tried to explain to me why I had to stay in hospital until I was well again. Now, as May progressed, I lost interest in my freedom. I ceased asking to go home, and I ceased trying to cooperate with Dr Jones and Mr Reese. I was now talking again and I didn't present as deranged anymore but, as Dr Jones told my father, I was still far from well, and certainly not well enough to be discharged.

The trouble is, Dr Jones explained to my father, when I was nine-years-old I had been sectioned and sent to St Lawrence's Hospital for five months. Then, when I was ten-years-old, my mother had committed me to the Attica asylum, where I languished for seven months until my father rescued me. Aged twelve in 1975 I had suffered another mental breakdown and spent my first spell of four months at Pen-y-Fal. Now, aged thirteen, I'd been at Pen-y-Fal for six months, including my brief sojourn to Hospital X. All in all, explained Dr Jones, that meant, roughly, I had spent two years out of the last five years of my young life in mental care. The result was I had lost that association with 'home' that was so important in a young person's development. I was estranged from my mother, and I no longer interacted with my sisters. I had started to bond to members of staff instead of my family, and I'd become too settled into institutional care of regulated days, little external pressures, regular meals and repetitive daily activities. All behind the locked doors of Ward 3.

One Thursday morning in mid-May my father came to visit me. However, before I was brought downstairs to the Visiting Room, Dr Jones appeared and asked my father to step into his office for a word.

'I think we have a problem with Alex,' said Dr Jones.

'Oh,' said my father, his heart sinking. 'I thought he was making progress.'

'He was, initially. But as I've already told you, I'm of the opinion that Alex has become too settled. He has ceased trying to get better. He is making no effort to meet me or Mr Reese even half-way, and he's obsessive about Nikki and Mark. That would be difficult for any youngster to cope with, but for Alex, in his weakened mental state, it's an almost insurmountable mountain to climb. It's becoming clear to me we're fighting a losing battle.

'Unless Alex makes an effort now, not in six months or next year, his future is, I regret to say, likely to become a long-term patient at Pen-y-Fal; initially on Ward 3 until his seventeenth birthday, and then perhaps indefinitely on an adult back-ward.'

'Surely not,' my father replied, quite shocked.

It seemed to him, he told me many years later, that my illness always took me three steps forwards and two steps back. He'd had quite enough of dealing with psychiatrists by now, and just wanted to see me well and living a normal life again.

'Is there nothing can be done?' my father asked.

'Well, there is something,' said Dr Jones. 'I would like you to sit down with Alex, and impress upon him that he must make an effort to meet us half-way. He *must* start making an effort to get well again if his future is not to be ruined by illness.'

My father mulled Dr Jones's words over for a moment before he gave an answer.

'Yes, Doctor,' he said. 'I can see what you say makes a lot of sense. I will have a heart-to-heart talk with Alex, but not here in hospital.'

'Oh,' said Dr Jones, 'where do you have in mind?'

'Well,' my Dad retorted with cunning, 'Alex likes cars and he always used to enjoy it when I took him out for a meal. I have just bought a new car, and I'm sure that will interest him. I think I should, with your permission, take him out for a ride in my car, and then stop off somewhere for lunch. Let him glimpse the outside world he is forfeiting by being a patient at Pen-y-Fal. If I use such a strategy, if I can tempt him with cars and a hamburger or two, he may be more receptive to my words of advice to cooperate with you and try to get better.'

Dr Jones sat back and digested my father's suggestion. Finally he nodded.

'Yes, Mr Sinclair,' he said. 'I think a few hours of day release for you to take Alex out to lunch would be a worthwhile exercise. Would you be willing to take him out today?'

'Yes,' replied my father. 'I'd like to take my son out today, if it's possible.'

The first I knew of this arrangement was when, instead of being summoned for my usual Thursday morning visit by my Dad in the Visiting Room, Mr Thomas told me to put my coat on, because my father had been given permission to take me out for a few hours.

I was stunned as Mr Thomas took me downstairs, there to find my father waiting for me in the foyer.

'Have a nice trip out, Alex,' said Mr Thomas, and he playfully patted my head before handing me over to my father.

'It's eleven o'clock now,' my father said. 'I've agreed with Dr Jones to bring Alex back by two o'clock.'

'Yes, that's correct,' said Mr Thomas. 'I'll expect him back on the ward by two.'

And with that my father took my arm and gestured for me to go with him, out the main door, out into the big wide world.

We went out to the car park, and I looked for my father's red Ford. Instead my Dad gestured to a brand new shiny silver Jaguar XJ6.

'Come on, Alex,' my father said happily. 'It's just the two of us for a few hours now, so get into my new car.'

I was very impressed by my Dad's new car, having always had a keen interest in anything automotive. It seemed so big and quiet.

My father powered his way up onto the wild countryside of Heads of the Valley Road, and the car effortlessly overtook everything that it came upon. We went twenty miles to Merthyr Tydfil, before my father turned the car around and headed back towards Abergavenny and the lush green countryside of Monmouthshire.

It was noon by the time we neared Abergavenny again, but my father had yet another surprise for me. Instead of taking me back to the hospital, he turned the car off the road into the car park of a *Little Chef* roadside cafe. He turned the engine off.

'Come on, Alex,' he said. 'I'm going to treat you to lunch. Would you like a hamburger and a Coca Cola?'

'Ooo, yes please, Dad,' I replied. And then I just sat in the car and stared at my hands in my lap.

'Well, what's the problem?' my father asked. 'Why don't you get out?'

'I was waiting for you to tell me I could,' I retorted.

My father gave me a sad sort of smile. He would one day long in the future tell me the word *institutionalised* sprang into his mind at that moment. I was actually sitting – waiting – for permission to open the door. My father could now see what Dr Jones had been alluding to. i.e. Not only was I not well enough to be discharged from Pen-y-Fal, but I had been there so long I was beginning to settle into an institutionalised way of life. Everything was done for me, my bed always made, my meals provided, the ward kept orderly. The nurses ruled supreme, but the price was I was beginning to not think for myself anymore.

'Of course you can get out, Alex,' my father said gently. 'Now come on. I'm sure you are as hungry as me, and we'll have two hamburgers each.'

I broke into a smile as I opened the door and got out.

It was a great adventure, in a small way, for me to enter a cafe and sit while my Dad ordered hamburgers, a Coca Cola for me, coffee for himself.

My father let me enjoy my treat before he tackled the real purpose of my trip out with him. To begin with he told me my grandmother was missing me, indeed he was missing me too, and it was time for me to make that final effort to convince Dr Jones to release me from Pen-y-Fal. Then he told me Dr Jones was very concerned that I was not making a greater effort to get better. Surely, my father said, I wanted to get better. It was not my destiny to remain at Pen-y-Fal forever. I had a life to lead, and the longer I stayed at Pen-y-Fal the harder it was going to be for me to pick up the threads of a normal life again once I was discharged.

Finally he paused for me to reply, but instead of a positive response all he got was a negative reaction.

'Please, Dad,' I said, 'I want to go back now. I want to go home.'

I couldn't have said a worse thing if I had done so wittingly.

'What do you mean by home?' my father asked.

'Hospital,' I replied. 'I want to go back to hospital now.'

'Haven't you been listening to me?' my father said, clearly annoyed. 'Pen-y-Fal is not your home. But it damn well will become so unless you make an effort to get better!'

'Please, Dad,' I said, my tears rising. 'I want to go back now.'

A young family and an elderly couple sat nearby turned to stare.

'Okay,' my father snapped, paying the bill. 'I'll take you back right now.'

Once outside in the car park I began to weep because, mentally weakened as I was, I didn't want my father to be angry with me. My father misunderstood my tears.

'Alex,' he said angrily, giving me a shake. 'Do you want to get better? Do you want to come back to live at home?'

'Yes,' I said, stifling a sob.

'Well, damn well pull yourself together, sonny. Dr Jones is annoyed with you and so am I. If you don't make an effort, and make that effort now, you're going to end up a full-time inmate at Pen-y-Fal. Are you listening to me?' he shouted.

'Yes,' I replied, and there could be no hiding my tears now.

'Pull yourself together. This is your last chance. If you don't make an effort to get better, I'm going to wash my hands of you,' he declared with a shout. 'You're going to end up in a mental hospital for good!'

By now I was distraught, sobbing and frantic, as my father unlocked the car and roughly shoved me in. He then got in, started the engine and revved it high in anger. With a squeal of tyres on tarmac, he raced out onto the main road.

My father said not another word to me all the way back to Pen-y-Fal. He swung in through the main gates, and raced up to the Children's Building.

Once in the foyer, he spoke to a secretary who telephoned the ward for a nurse to come down for me.

When Mr Thomas came down, all my father said was: 'Goodbye, Alex.' And there was many a meaning – and an air of finality – to the way he said it.

'Dad,' I cried. 'I'll make an effort to get better, I promise.'

My father looked at me for a long moment, then just nodded his head as Mr Thomas took me away.

I was not to know it that day, but even as Mr Thomas took me back to the ward, even as I took myself off to lie on my bed crying because I knew my father was angry with me, my father was meeting with Dr Jones.

In a way I am fortunate, for what my father didn't tell me at the time, I was to learn many years later when he told me the complete story of my breakdown in 1977.

My father explained to the doctor what had happened. He explained all had seemed to go well, until I had actually asked to return to Pen-y-Fal.

'I was afraid of this,' said Dr Jones. 'Alex has been in hospital so long now that he has become too settled, too ready to accept the daily regime on the ward. He's been in hospital now for six months. Normally, I wouldn't expect a patient to become so settled in such a time, but in Alex's weakened mental state after what happened to him in Greece, the regime on the ward, the regularity of meals, wash-time, bed-time, life here is about as much as he can cope with. If you were to put him into an unfamiliar environment, I don't think he'd be able to handle it, and what you saw today was an example of this. He became frightened out of his ward environment, and he actually *asked* you to bring him back. That's a bad sign, but it gives me a direction to approach his treatment.

'As awkward and unpleasant as the experience was for Alex, I would ask if you could take him out for lunch twice a week from now on. We will have to work together; me to treat him for his psychosis and PTSD; you to interrupt the way he has become too settled on the ward. A trip out twice a week for lunch should re-educate the way he thinks of the world. Despite the setback that Alex got upset today, I think he has taken a small but significant step on the road to recovery.'

The Abba tune *Waterloo* droned onto the ward from the nurses' office, and it seemed to me that the nurses always had their radio on, and always some tune or other by Abba echoed down the corridor to the Day Room.

The music on Ward 3 is one of my clear memories of that time, as is my memory of Mr Thomas standing out on the fire-escape to have a cigarette. Smoking was a popular habit amongst the staff on the ward, and whilst it would draw comment nowadays, in the 1970s it was not remarkable in any way.

Those two things – Abba music and the nurses smoking out on the fire-escape – are clear in my memory, as are the key events I have recalled in this book. However it is pertinent to mention that my psychosis and the ECT also damaged my memory, so certain events from the winter of 1976 and the spring of 1977 are entirely lost to me. Other key events, however, were burnt into my memory, never to be forgotten, and in a way I suppose I'm fortunate. As I ever so slowly recovered from my psychosis, so my memory began to recover too.

By late May Dr Jones had my condition largely under control, and my mental equilibrium seemed much more balanced. I was still seeing Mr Reese every other day at 2:30 for an hour of therapy, and at these meetings he'd ask me how I was feeling: Why had I been crying again? Did I still believe I had killed Nikki and Mark? Had I heard Dr Schultz talking to me again?

I knew Mr Reese and Dr Jones were trying to help me, but I also knew my father was angry with me for not making enough effort to get better. The result was

I started lying to Mr Reese and Dr Jones. When asked if I'd been hearing voices, I shook my head and said 'no.' When asked about Nikki and Mark, I was now able to hold back my tears. I'd stare at my feet, avoiding Mr Reese's eyes, and say I was 'sorry they'd died.' Then determination would grip me and I'd assert it *was* my fault they'd died. With regards to Nikki, Mr Reese was dubious about my claims. In the case of Mark, he couldn't deny I'd been to blame. There had been an inquest by now, and half a dozen witnesses had given evidence that asserted I had caused Mark to run into the road. I had thus got him killed. The Coroner's verdict was not even an Accident; it was recorded as Misadventure. i.e. It was declared as a mishap, and I felt I was not entirely free of blame.

Over that stumbling block Mr Reese would subside into silence, eventually to say: 'Alex, regardless of the Coroner's verdict, Mark's death *was* an accident. Please try to be a little kinder to yourself. Blaming yourself will not bring him back you know.' And with that he would get up, open his office door, and take me back to the ward.

This was now my weekly ordeal on Mondays, Wednesdays and Fridays. After lunch I had to face Mr Reese and his 'therapy' as he tried to make me leap my mental hurdles of self-blame and hate.

My only respite now came in the form of my father. He changed his visiting days to Wednesday and Saturday mornings. Now, instead of the Visiting Room, every time he came he took me out in the car. Sometimes he took me to the town of Monmouth, sometimes to Ebbw Vale, other times to Tredegar, sometimes even into Abergavenny, but never via Monk Street. In these towns he'd park the car and we'd wander the high street, looking in shop windows, and always we'd conclude our visit at a cafe for lunch, where my father would order bacon and eggs, sausages and chips, or any type of food he knew I enjoyed.

To start with I found these twice weekly trips out an ordeal. I'd been in hospital so long by now I found the noise of a high street hard to cope with. I just wasn't used to the crowds and bustle. I also couldn't judge the speed of the traffic when we had to cross the road. Everything seemed to move so quickly. Thus, whilst I enjoyed my mornings out with my father and the variation of lunch with him, to begin with I found the whole experience very stressful.

As for my father, he would later tell me he had enjoyed his trips out with me. He finally felt he was doing something to help me get better. This after six months of inactivity and frustration whilst he sat at home fifty miles from me incarcerated in a psychiatric hospital. It was this newfound experience of trying to help his mentally ill son that gave my father confidence that he could accomplish as much to cure me as my psychiatrist. Yes, Dr Jones doled out my medication, which my father could not. Yes, Dr Jones had the benefit of thirty years' experience as a psychiatrist, which my father did not. And finally, yes, Dr Jones had the backup of all the resources at Pen-y-Fal to aid him, whilst my father was an amateur in anything to do with mental health.

However, my father was a very determined sort of man, and nothing ever determined him quite so much as saving his only son. Thus my father spent a fortnight reading every book on psychiatry and psychology he could find, in an effort to understand the nature of my illness and so be able to make a contribution towards my recovery. My father knew he could not do anything connected to drugs. Psychiatric drugs were Dr Jones's domain and my father could not stray into uncharted territory. However, the sort of therapy and good practical psychoanalysis Mr Reese practiced my father was sure he could manage.

And so it was that on my twice weekly trips out with my father, he would talk about himself and his past, and then, gently, encourage me to talk about the things that had happened to me. To begin with he encouraged me to talk about my life on the ward, about my friends and experiences. Then, subtly, he encouraged me to talk about events from the past.

My father began to realise that all my traumas of the past had mounted up to make me frightened of facing the present. I confided to him – made him swear to keep my secret – that I believed I was being haunted by Nikki. I often heard him talking, I said.

My father finally began to understand my mental problems. These hallucinations were an imbalance of the brain, most likely triggered by trauma and years of abuse inflicted on me by my mother. That illness he could do nothing about. It would have to be managed by Dr Jones.

My Post Traumatic Stress Disorder, my paranoia that I'd got Nikki and Mark killed, my father believed he could help me with. It would involve a lot of talking therapy as he let me, finally, unburden my soul of the guilt I felt over their deaths. My belief that I was being haunted by Nikki, because in my less lucid moments I could hear him, was more difficult to manage. However, my father was sure that once I'd unburdened myself of the guilt, so too would my belief that I was being haunted by Nikki vanish too. My father did not believe in such things as haunting. He came to the conclusion that if I could be cured of my traumas of the past, so too would my mental health improve and I would recover, never to be ill again.

Cure the trauma, went my father's logic, cure the child. My father began to plot how to put his scheme into practice. Dr Jones could dispense pills. Only he, my father believed, could dispense peace of mind and reconciliation with the past to his only son.

# CHAPTER 9

# Truth

Psychoanalysis, of the sort practiced by Mr Reese, is a complex form of talking therapy with no drug involvement. I suppose in all my years of childhood illness about every type of psychoanalysis, from cognitive behavioural therapy and free association through to the more complex and deep psychological treatments of Dr Schultz, were practiced on me. In May of 1977, seeing Mr Reese every other afternoon for an hour, he touched on virtually every kind of treatment, including drawing complex diagrams such as about the relationship between me and my mother (which he called the 'big figure'), and me and my father (which he called the 'small figure,' because my father had up to now played a lesser role in my upbringing).

My father's warning to me to make an effort to get better had much effect, and I, cornered with no avenue of escape, realised that the only way to keep my father's devotion was to ensure Dr Jones discharged me within a few months. I didn't think I could keep my father's love and attention much beyond August. I therefore had eight weeks to, in Dr Jones's words, be 'kind to myself' and present as if I was recovered. As far as I was aware, never told anything by Dr Jones or Mr Reese, my strategy was working.

In a cycle of improvement, the better I got, the clearer my thoughts. The clearer my thoughts, the better I got. I began to feel more optimistic about the future.

During the latter half of May and into the first week of June, my father came to take me out every Wednesday and Saturday. We visited many towns to wander the shops and have lunch out, before my father returned me to the ward at 2:00 p.m. However, it was no longer just a matter of just taking me out, for my father, now well-read on psychoanalysis, wanted to try the talking cure on me as well.

One Saturday he picked me up as usual and took me out. We only went as far as Abergavenny on this occasion and, sat in the Jaguar in a car park, my father asked if I'd help him with a 'little experiment,' a word game. Keen to keep my Dad's love, I agreed.

'It's a very simple game,' my father explained. 'It's word association. I'll say a word and you say the first thing that comes into your mind.'

Oh, I thought, Mr Reese has already tried this one on me. Okay, if Dad wants to play, I'm game.

However, word association is no game and should not be played with.

'Okay, Dad,' I said. 'I'll play the word game with you.'

To start with my father kept the game simple.

'Cow,' he said.

'Field,' I replied.

'Farm,' he said.

'Chickens,' I replied.

'Chickens,' he said.

'Eggs,' was my reply.

We sat in the car for the next fifteen minutes with Dad saying his simple words, and I gave a genuine answer, but my father had no intention of keeping this game simple...

'Greece,' he said.

'Attica,' I replied.

'Attica,' he said.

'Fear,' I replied, beginning to feel nervous.

'Fear,' he said.

'Nikki,' I replied, feeling my heart rate speeding up.

'Nikki,' said Dad.

'Death,' I replied, and by now I was as frightened as if I were on a rollercoaster ride that would not stop.

'Death!' said my father sharply.

'Me!' I exclaimed in anguish. 'Oh, please stop, Dad. I don't want to play anymore. Oh God help me, please stop!' And I broke down in tears.

My father looked deeply shocked at my reply, and immediately put a consoling arm out to hug me.

'It's okay, Alex. It's okay,' he said gently. 'We won't play anymore.'

He sat back and lit his pipe, whilst I composed myself, but I knew he was shocked by my answer because I could see his hands were shaking. The 'word game' had become deadly serious and, I think, my father suddenly realised how dangerous words and psychoanalysis could be in the wrong hands.

Once my upset had subsided we got out of the car, and Dad promised me lunch as a treat in a local cafe.

As we walked up the high street to the cafe my father put a tender arm about me.

'Alex,' he said, 'you're deeply troubled by your memories, aren't you?'

106

'I suppose so,' I replied glumly.

'Why are you now frightened of Nikki?' he asked. 'He was your friend. He'd never harm you.'

'I'm frightened,' I said, 'because Nikki is waiting for me, and I don't know what he wants. Perhaps he's angry I let him die. I didn't mean to let Nikki die, Dad, honestly I didn't. Sometimes I can see him standing nearby in the corner of my eye, but when I turn to look he vanishes. Other times I can hear his voice, but I don't understand what he's saying because he's talking Greek.'

My father looked serious at my revelation. Perhaps, he thought, the 'word game' had worked, because I was now really emphasising my worst fears. Something I had never mentioned to Dr Jones or Mr Reese: my darkest fear that Nikki was 'waiting' for me. My father began to realise how troubled I really was, and he was sure that a cure for my fear would not come from Dr Jones or Mr Reese. It was at that moment, an embryonic moment, walking up the street with his arm about me, that the seeds of an idea began to germinate in his mind. The concept my father thought of had the potential to banish fear from my mind, but it was a high-risk strategy. If he failed I might never be cured. If he was caught, the police and the judiciary would throw the book at him.

My father now determined to take my cure into his own hands. He recognised Dr Jones was a clever paediatric psychiatrist, and he had prescribed me drugs that undoubtedly had got my psychosis under control. I was currently in the best environment. I was safe and secure, with kind nurses who looked after me. I even had friends my own age in the ward. But in the long run my future must not be to become a long-term inmate at Pen-y-Fal. My father began to plot. He knew it was a high-risk strategy, and Dr Jones and Mr Reese would be furious with him, but I was his son, and my father believed he had a genuine right to take my cure and recovery into his own hands. He began to make arrangements, knowing he intended to put his plan into action the following weekend.

Tuesday, 7 June 1977, was my fourteenth birthday, and my father arranged to come to visit me that morning. Birthdays were always a big event on the ward, for the other boys all made me birthday cards, and Nurse Johnson was determined to keep her charges happy and encourage fun. My father came to see me early that morning in the Visiting Room, and I can remember how disappointed I was when he told me he wasn't going to take me out.

'No,' said my Dad. 'I'll just visit you here today, because I want to see Dr Jones this morning to ask him if he will grant you home leave next weekend.'

At the mention of going home for the weekend my eyes went like saucers.

'Ooo, yes please,' I exclaimed. 'I'd like to stay at Nanny's for a day or two.'

'Good,' said my father, producing a present from his pocket. 'Now open your birthday present. I had to keep it small because you're in hospital, but as soon as you come home I'll buy you something more exciting.'

I eagerly tore the wrapping paper off, and found inside a plush box. I opened the box and within it lay a shiny new digital Timex watch. It was very smart, and so modern, digital watches being something of a novelty in the 1970s.

'Thank you, Dad,' I said, giving him a hug. 'It's perfect; just what I wanted.'

My father smiled, and with that Nurse Clark popped her head around the door to tell me it was time I went back to the ward, and that Dr Jones was now ready to see my father.

I gave my father a parting hug, and then hurried back to the ward to show Kevin my birthday present.

As soon as I returned to the ward I sought Kevin out in the Day Room, where everyone was waiting for Mrs Howell to arrive to give us morning lessons.

By now Christopher had moved on, his parents and Social Services having secured a place for him at a children's home in Hereford. Christopher would never again be allowed to pose a threat to his younger sister, and as far as I could see his childhood had been ruined by one impulsive act of madness.

Kevin, on the other hand, had now become my best friend, and we'd become very close.

Kevin was lucid and bright that day. Dr Jones had got his medication balance correct, and Kevin was getting better really quickly. He immediately took an interest in my present, as I proudly displayed it on my wrist.

'Coo,' said Kevin. 'Like your watch. How does it work?'

We spent the next twenty minutes closely examining it, even reading the instruction leaflet to discover how to set and display the calendar function.

Later that day, after tea, Nurse Johnson produced a birthday cake she had brought in for me, and everyone sang happy birthday before I blew out the candle and cut the cake.

'Remember to make a wish,' said Judy.

As I plunged the knife into the cake, I made a secret wish: I wished my father would come to take me home soon. I wished never to be mentally ill again, and then I'd never have to come back to Pen-y-Fal.

After I cut the cake Nurse Johnson took the knife off me and skilfully cut the cake into twenty-four slices, enough for every boy and nurse on the ward.

As I was munching my cake and chatting happily to Kevin, Judy appeared at my side and handed me a present wrapped in bright paper.

'Happy birthday, Alex,' she said. 'I hope you enjoy your presents, and may your every wish come true.'

I eagerly unwrapped my present, and with joy found it contained an Asterix cartoon book. There were several copies on the ward, but this was a title I'd not seen before: *Asterix and Cleopatra.*

'Thank you!' I exclaimed, and gave Judy a kiss. 'Thank you, very much.'

'That's okay,' Judy replied. 'Just you keep on getting better.'

'Yes, I'll try.' I said.

Given the circumstances I had a really nice birthday and, after eating our cake, Kevin and I went to lie upon my bed and read together the latest funny adventure of Asterix. I can still remember to this day Kevin's giggles, and our shrieks of laughter that echoed joyfully down the ward corridor. It was the happiest evening I ever had at Pen-y-Fal.

Medication was dispensed at 8:00 p.m., and then everyone was in bed by 9:30 p.m. 'Lights out' took place, and Kevin and I lay chatting in the dark, Kevin having to repeatedly smother his laughter with his pillow lest we both got into trouble for talking at a time when we were supposed to be asleep.

I suppose wishes can come true, but for me never in a way that was usually expected.

On the morning following my birthday, Nurse Johnson took me aside and told me that my father had been given permission to take me home for three days next weekend. My 'home-leave' was to start next Friday morning, and I could go home – to my grandmother's house – until Monday morning.

'Now remember,' warned Nurse Johnson, 'Dr Jones is placing his faith in you. We don't want to hear you've been frantic, and,' she said, tapping my hand, 'we don't want to find you've bitten yourself again. If your home-leave is a success, then you can have some more weekends at home. It will by your first step on the road to discharge from the ward. Do you promise to make an effort?'

'Yes,' I replied. 'I'll try very hard to be perfect.'

'You don't need to be perfect,' said Nurse Johnson, shaking her head in exasperation. 'Just be you. No one expects miracles of you, Alex. Just try to stay calm.'

I promised and assured Nurse Johnson I'd make a special effort to be good, and then I hurried off to find Kevin and tell him my wonderful news.

Having been told I could go home for the weekend, Wednesday and Thursday seemed to really drag, especially morning lessons with Mrs Howell. However, I had Kevin to cheer me up and it seemed that when we were together we were forever giggling and laughing, and Kevin's happy personality kept my moral up and I was happy too.

Friday finally came, and I sat on my bed while I waited for my father to arrive, holding my anorak on my lap and kicking my heels against the floor as I chatted to Kevin.

Eventually Kevin broached a subject that was bothering him. He told me he was having nightmares in which he was being chased.

'Do you think I should tell Dr Jones?' he asked anxiously with a sideways glance.

It was clear to me that Kevin was not quite so bright and happy that day, and his problems were really bothering him. I mulled Kevin's question over.

'Look,' I said, 'we're both stuck in Pen-y-Fal because we're not well. Don't keep your nightmares a secret. You know I have nightmares too, and to help me Dr Jones prescribed me some tablets to help me sleep. Perhaps he will give you the same pills. You don't want nasty dreams if you can help it.'

I looked sideways at Kevin as he slowly nodded his head.

'Yes,' he said finally. 'I'll tell Dr Jones. Perhaps a pill at night might help me.'

Nurse Clark appeared and stuck her head around the dormitory door.

'Alex,' she called. 'Your father's here.'

I gave Kevin a playful punch on the shoulder, and hurriedly pulled on my anorak as I left the dorm, heading to my father and a weekend of fun. A weekend of sleeping in my own room and watching whatever I wanted on the television. Perhaps to even go out to the seaside town of Penarth on Saturday afternoon for a stroll on the pier and an ice-cream.

Yes, I thought as I hurried down the stairs, a weekend of fun lay ahead of me.

My father met me and Nurse Clark in the foyer, and nodded when the nurse said I was expected to be back on the ward by noon on Monday. Yes, my father assured her, he'd have me back without fail, and with that he opened the door for me and I headed off for my first weekend of home leave.

My father's car swiftly overtook cars and lorries on the highway to Newport, where it joined the motorway between London and Cardiff. I was now puzzled, for my father turned in the wrong direction, heading east towards London. However, my father was full of chat as he drove, and then he revealed he'd got a big surprise for me.

'We're not going to Cardiff,' he confided, to my astonishment. 'I've booked us on a flight to Italy out of Heathrow Airport at 2:30 p.m.'

'Italy?' I gasped. 'I thought I was supposed to be staying at Nanny's until Monday.'

'Oh, I think you can forget Monday,' my father replied. 'We're not due back until Wednesday.'

'Wednesday!' I exclaimed. 'Won't Dr Jones be angry with me if I'm not back on Monday?'

'Look, Alex,' said my father, 'I'm taking you on a short holiday to Rome. I would think you'd be happy. Surely you don't want to be back in hospital by Monday afternoon, do you?'

'No,' I said. Then resolve hardened within me. My Dad was taking me on a foreign holiday. Precisely why, I didn't know. But I was sure it would be fun. 'Won't I need some clothes?' I asked.

'I've got your case packed in the boot,' my father replied, 'and in four hours we'll be on a plane heading for Rome. Doesn't that excite you?'

'Yes, Dad, very much,' I said. 'We're going to have a great time, I'm sure.'

However, even as I said it I pondered Dr Jones's reaction. I was sure I would get into trouble. Surely there would be repercussions. I left these worries unspoken.

The fight from Heathrow landed at Rome's Fiumicino Airport at 5:45 p.m., and Dad and I were soon out of the busy airport, cases in hand, and stood in a queue at a taxi rank in the evening heat of an Italian summer.

By now I was dressed in summer clothes for a hot climate, which I'd put on in the car once we'd arrived at Heathrow. Now I wore only sandals, shorts and a t-shirt.

We arrived at the front of the queue, and a man opened the boot of a Fiat taxi to take our luggage. I climbed into the back seat, my father sat next to the driver.

'Where to?' the cab driver asked in faultless English.

'*Hotel Romero*, Via delle Terme di Tito,' my father replied.

The driver stuck his arm out of the window, the cab charged out into the traffic, and soon we were on the main highway into Rome, passing groves of oranges and olives.

Twenty minutes later we were in the suburbs of Rome, and the traffic was horrendous, with commuters and taxis driving with the ferocity of rats at the kill. Show no mercy seemed to be the rules of the road in Rome. I gazed out of the window in fascination at a ruin here, the odd ancient column there, all tucked in between modern buildings.

'Quick, Alex,' said my father, gesturing to the right. 'Look, it's the Roman Forum.'

I gazed at a landscape of monumental ruins and tufts of dry grass.

The most spectacular sight for me came a few moments later when the cab rounded the Coliseum, and I was staggered at its size. I'd seen pictures of the Coliseum in books, but nothing could have prepared me for its sheer bulk and imposing nature.

Suddenly the cab swerved through the traffic, and angry motorists sounded their horns as the cab cut across their paths to enter a street just off the Coliseum. It stopped before the *Hotel Romero*.

That evening my father took me out to a small restaurant, where we sat outside at a table in the street and ate spaghetti Bolognese, my Dad washing his meal down with a carafe of red wine, me with a Coca Cola. After our meal, by now 9:30 p.m., my Dad and I wandered the streets in the sultry heat of Rome in early summer. We walked 200 yards beyond our hotel, and there before us was the Coliseum all floodlight at night, and still there was an endless stream of traffic surrounding it.

'Would you like to see inside it?' my father asked.

'Yes please, Dad.' I replied.

'Good,' came the reply, 'Then you shall. And you shall see the Vatican, the Roman Forum, and the ruined palaces of the Emperors.' My father put an arm across my shoulders. 'But now,' he said, 'I think you've had a long day, and it's time you went to bed.'


The knock on the hotel room door woke me from a light slumber. I lay on my bed, feeling the sultry heat of an Italian summer morning already making the day oppressively hot. There was another knock on the door, and a voice called: 'Permitto?'

'Avante!' my father replied, and the door opened to admit a waiter who wheeled in a breakfast trolley.

'La prima callazione, Signor,' the waiter said, and wheeled the trolley to two seats by the French windows that overlooked the verdant gardens across the Terme di Tito.

My father and I sat down to breakfast of orange juice and freshly baked bread rolls smothered in bright yellow Tuscany butter, and all the while I stared at the Terme di Tito gardens.

Down in the street there was a lion's head fountain set into a wall from which bubbled and gurgled sweet cold water. That, my father told me was called the *Fontana di via delle Terme di Tito.*

Having taken my Haloperidol and dressed in shorts and t-shirt, and armed with my camera thoughtfully placed in my suitcase by my father, we set off to explore Rome.

We walked to the Coliseum, where my father flagged down a passing cab. Boarding the ubiquitous Fiat 124, my father told the driver to take us to the Piazza Farnese. Once again, I saw traffic driven the Roman way, with no mercy given to any mistake by another driver. Horns blared continuously, and drivers leant out of their windows to gesticulate and shout at each other in the bright June sunshine.

Dropped off at the entrance to the Piazza Farnese, my Dad and I found ourselves in a sea of tranquillity amongst the blare and chaos of Roman traffic. It was a short walk across the Piazza to the imposing Farnese Palace, which served as the French Embassy.

Showing his passport to the Embassy doorman, we were soon in the cool of a vast entrance foyer. My father went up to the receptionist's desk.

'Pierre Caval, Military Attaché,' said my father.

'Who shall I say is asking for him?' the woman asked.

'Peter Sinclair,' he replied.

The receptionist was instantly on the telephone, and soon a man in his late thirties came tripping lightly down a vast marble staircase.

'Peter!' Pierre exclaimed. 'How nice to see you. The last time we met it was in Cairo. How did you find me?'

'Oh, I made a few enquiries,' my father replied. 'I'm here on holiday with my son, and I thought I'd look you up. I want to ask you some questions about the Egyptian military.'

'How are things in Cairo?' Pierre asked, suddenly serious. He gestured to a sofa in a corner of the foyer. 'Come, we must sit and talk.'

My father, who was acting as the secret envoy between the Israeli and Egyptian governments, was suddenly serious too.

'Yes, we must talk,' he replied.

My father looked at me for a long moment, then said: 'You can wait for me outside, Alex. Pierre and I will be a while. Why don't you go down that corridor and out into the garden. Can you to do that for me?' he asked, a serious expression on his face.

This was a side to my father I'd never seen before. At home he was a weak man who usually gave in to my mother, which had ultimately resulted in catastrophic consequences for me. Now, standing before me stood a hardened professional, and a diplomatic envoy. I determined not to let him down at such an important moment. I realised my father's conversation with Pierre Caval was more important than me. I agreed to go out into the garden.

Freedom! I thought, that my father was willing to trust me to go outside on my own for a while.

'I'll expect you back in half an hour,' my father said. 'Can I trust you, Alex?'

'Yes, you can trust me, Dad,' I responded. 'I'll be back in precisely half an hour.' And off I headed on my adventure.

Half an hour's freedom without supervision, and no one to escort or guard me. I got to walk in the tranquil and empty Farnese Gardens all by myself, and I was so excited I can still remember my little adventure to this day. I walked paths, I even climbed a tree and peered down over a high wall into the bustle of a street beyond, and all the while I was thinking to myself that I must be getting better mentally for my Dad to trust me to go out on my own, in a city as big as Rome. I knew I would always have PTSD, but my psychosis was now under control, and I could be myself again, an interesting child full of curiosity. My sojourn to Rome, and to be let loose in the Eternal City all on my own, I thought, must mean my Dad considered me almost cured as well.

Within half an hour I was back at the entrance to the French Embassy, sat on the steps awaiting my father's return. He soon appeared, looking all serious and business-like, but on spotting me his face lit up and all seriousness vanished.

'Well, Alex,' he said, 'that's the business side of my trip over. Now it's just you and me and our holiday. Did you enjoy your walk in the Farnese Gardens?'

'Yes, Dad,' I replied. 'Very much.'

'Good,' he said. 'I think that little bit of independence is a sign you're recovering. A month ago I wouldn't have dreamt of letting you go out on your own. It's a sign your getting better, sonny.' And with that he playfully ruffled my hair.

Yes, I thought, I am getting better, because a month ago I'd have been too frightened to go out on my own.

My walk in the Farnese Gardens became a defining moment in my recovery. I rarely heard 'voices' anymore, and my cognitive abilities were swiftly being restored. I suppose it was at that moment I proved to myself that I really was getting better, my sanity returning, and it was in no small part due to my solitary walk in the beautiful gardens behind the French Embassy.

'Come on, Alex,' said my father. 'It's time we were on our way to the Vatican.'

He flagged down a passing cab.

Dropped off at the entrance to the Vatican City, my father quickly led me through the crowds into the vast space of St Peter's Square.

'Now be careful!' my father commanded. 'If you lose sight of me or get lost, just stop and stay where you are, or I may never find you again.'

'Yes, Dad,' I replied.

After six months in hospital, all peace and tranquillity, a stable environment, I found the sight and sound of the vast crowds truly unsettling. I made sure I kept my father in sight, and when pressed in upon by hoards of tourists, all eager to see the sights and snapping wildly at every novelty with their cameras, I clung onto my father's jacket. There was no way I wanted to get lost in Rome. I just don't think it ever occurred to my father that I'd find all this hustle and bustle so stressful.

By 11:30 a.m. the heat of the summer sun was beating mercilessly down on St Peter's Square, so it was with some relief that we entered the cool and tranquillity of St Peter's Basilica. We wandered the magnificent basilica, looked at statues of long-dead saints, and watched as a party of nuns walked up one aisle, a group of monks down the other.

'Truly,' said my father in a hushed tone, and brought up Church of England, 'this must be the epicentre of Christianity.'

I thought for a long moment, mulling over the weight of my Dad's words, and agreed. I took in all the majesty and grace of the basilica, and was truly impressed.

Next we visited the Sistine Chapel, and gazed in wonder up at the ceiling paintings by Michelangelo.

We were quite finished with the Vatican by 1:00 p.m., and my father announced it was time to find some lunch.

We departed the Vatican on foot, back into the mayhem of Rome, when suddenly my father grabbed my arm and dragged me over to see something he'd just spotted.

'Look, Alex,' he said, his eyes twinkling with humour.

I looked, and began to smile as well.

Amongst all the high culture of the Vatican, the splendour of ancient Roman ruins, the posh shops of Gucci and Armani, stood an incongruous little man with a cart before him selling hotdogs. Plastered on a brightly coloured parasol and down both sides of his cart were images of the American flag, pictures of the Empire State Building and the Statue of Liberty.

'Come on,' said my father, and we joined a waiting queue.

Fifteen minutes later we were stood in the shade of a building eating American style hotdogs. Then, once we'd finished lunch, we sought out a cafe that sold a soft drink for me and a coffee for my father.

It is said by the inhabitants of Rome that only tourists are crazy enough to venture out into the midday heat of a Roman summer, and I think they are correct. The sun beat down mercilessly and the heat was reflected off the sizzling hot pavements. Determined not to be defeated by the sun, my father went to a street vendor and bought a hat for himself and a peaked sailor's cap for me. Then my father grabbed my arm in one hand and, with a street map in the other, we set off on a marathon walk across central Rome to see the ruins of the Forum.

Once we arrived in the vast area that composed the ruins of the ancient Forum of Rome, my father gave me quite an expert tour. We visited the tumbled masonry of the Temple of Castor and Pollux, the Temple of Jupiter, the old dilapidated Senate House (in which some of the great decisions of ancient history were taken) and the Arch of Septimus Severus. This tour took the rest of the afternoon and I was by now flagging, plodding along further and further behind my father. My father stopped and came back.

'Are you alright, Alex?' he asked.

'Yes, Dad,' I replied. 'It's just my legs and feet ache so much.'

'You're right,' he said. 'I forgot you've been in hospital six months. You're not used to walking such long distances. I'm sorry, you must be very tired by now. Come, let's go and sit in the nearby *Gardens de la Villa Celimontana*.'

And with that he put a tender arm around my shoulders and led me slowly back down the Forum to the *Gardens de la Villa Celimontana*, where we sat upon the ground in the shade of a tree in the heat of an Italian afternoon.

Despite my fatigue I was enjoying myself enormously. The power and majesty of Rome, the magnificent ruins, the beautiful gardens, all made a great impression on me. It was as if my father's idea of taking me to Rome was very therapeutic. I can remember thinking all this has been waiting for me to get out of hospital to see. I felt a qualm of conscience to think what I'd put my Dad through when I'd been ill.

'I'm sorry I've been such a nuisance, Dad,' I said suddenly.

'That's okay, Alex,' my father replied. 'You've been very ill, and it couldn't have been helped.'

'I swear to make a supreme effort to get better,' I said. 'And then I'll never be ill again.'

'Good boy,' said my father with a smile. 'I always knew you had it in you to get better, despite what all the doctors said. Now you must rest. We have to get up at dawn tomorrow. You must be fit and well, well in mind and well in body, for tomorrow I am going to set you off on the road to a full recovery.'

I pondered my father's words, and wondered what he had in mind. I kept my questions to myself, and sat back against the tree.

That evening my father took me out again to the small restaurant where we sat outside eating cannelloni. This time my father poured a small quantity of red wine from his carafe into my glass and proposed a toast.

'To your recovery, Alex,' he said.

And with that he drank his wine and gestured for me to do the same.

For the first time in my life I drank wine, and found it a fulsome, if not curious tasting experience.

As I lay in bed that evening, my Dad outside at the hotel's terrace bar with his favourite tipple of whisky on ice, I pondered again what my father had in mind, and what did he mean when he'd said he'd be setting me on the road to a *full* recovery? With these thoughts swirling in my mind, I eventually drifted off into my usual fitful sleep.

I could feel someone shaking my shoulder as I lay asleep. I tried to ignore the shaking, but the hand was determined to wake me. I awoke to the sound of my father calling me.

'Alex... Alex... Wake up. It's time we were on our way.'

I opened bleary eyes to see my father stood by the side of my bed. He had already shaved and dressed. I blinked in the electric lighting, then noticed it was still dark beyond the French windows.

'What time is it, Dad?' I asked, bewildered as to why my father wanted me up and dressed.

'It's five o'clock,' he said. 'Come on, its time you were up. We have to be on our way.'

'Five o'clock?' I repeated. 'Crumbs. Why do we have to get up so early?'

'It's a surprise,' said my father. 'And it's the real reason I've brought you to Rome. Now have a quick wash and get dressed. We must be on our way in ten minutes.'

I quickly went to the bathroom, douched my face in cold water and brushed my teeth, hurriedly dressed in shirt, shorts and sandals, all accomplished in under ten minutes. I took my tablets.

'Good,' said my father. 'Let's be on our way.'

He hustled me out of our room, and within minutes we were stood in the street outside the hotel.

I looked at my Dad, wondering if he knew where he was going.

'Come on,' he said, turning right and heading towards the Coliseum.

We reached the Coliseum in just a few minutes, and I was surprised how peaceful and quiet it was, with no traffic surrounding it in this last half hour before the sun rose heralding another hot sunny day. For the first time I saw the Coliseum at peace with itself, belying its gruesome past. We crossed the road, and my father led me up a long series of steps onto the Palatine Hill. It was a long climb up to where the ruins of the Roman palaces of the Caesars lay, all dilapidated and tumbled down.

The view across the city was magnificent, and I could even look down at the scattered remains of the Circus Maximus in the valley below, its shape outlined by the glow of streetlights. Far to the east the black sky was beginning to turn orange, hinting that dawn was not far off.

'Oh, Dad,' I whispered, as if one should not break the tranquillity of the moment, 'it's wonderful. Is this what you wanted to show me?'

'No,' said my father, suddenly serious. 'We haven't much time. Now come on.'

He led me through the ruins, and soon we were on another set of steps descending from the Palatine to the valley below. To my left I could see the Circus Maximus, and the Roman Forum behind me to my right. A quaint little church with a high tower was in the valley before us.

'Come on,' said my father, heading across the road to the church. 'This is what we've come to Rome to see.'

He led me around to the front of the church, and I looked up at its seven-storey tower. My father put a guiding hand into the small of my back, and propelled me up the steps into a dimly lit portico.

We stood in the portico for some minutes, letting our eyes adjust to the darkness. It was then that I saw it: a huge marble disk stood against the wall, easily a foot taller than my father. Carved onto the disk was the enormous face of a man, with holes for eyes and mouth, a mane of flowing hair encircling his face.

'This is the *Bocca della Verità*,' said my father, 'the "Mouth of Truth." Before you is the face of the Roman god Oceanus. The most famous feature of this carving is the mouth. It is an ancient lie detector. If you place your hand into the mouth and tell a lie, it will bite your hand off.'

I could feel the hair on the nape of my neck begin to prickle.

'Is this what we've come to Rome to see?' I asked.

'Yes,' my father answered. 'See, and more.'

He solemnly took off his hat, and placed his hand in Oceanus's mouth.

'Oh, Oceanus,' he said, summoning up the spirit of the ancient god, 'I stand here before you and proclaim that I love my son, Alexander, more than any other living being.'

He paused a moment, then slowly drew his hand out of the mouth.

'Come on, Alex,' he said. 'Now it's your turn.'

'Please, Dad,' I pleaded, 'don't make me do this. I'm scared.'

'Nonsense,' said my father. 'Now put your hand into the mouth.'

Trembling, I placed my hand into the cold marble mouth, ready to snatch it out again at the first hint of a bite.

'Alex,' said my father, 'you understand you must tell the truth with your hand in the mouth of old Oceanus.'

'Yes, Dad,' I replied, quite terrified by now.

'Okay,' said my father. 'Tell me why you're afraid of Nikki.'

'I let him die,' I replied.

'How did he die?'

'He suffered a fit, and then he choked to death when he swallowed his tongue.'

'Did you kill Nikki?'

I gulped.

'Yes,' I replied. 'I got him locked in isolation with me as punishment. In there we began to fight, until finally he collapsed in an epileptic fit. He swallowed his tongue and died with me holding him. If I hadn't fought with him, he wouldn't have had the fit, and he wouldn't have died.'

By now tears were welling up in my eyes, but I so much didn't want to cry in front of my father, not now I'd taken yesterday's decision that I wanted to get better. Tears would be a sign of weakness.

'Alex,' said my father, his voice firm and commanding, 'do you trust me?'

'Yes, Dad,' I answered.

'Good. Then I want you to repeat after me "I did not kill Nikki. His death was an accident."'

'Oh, Dad,' I cried, 'if I say that old Oceanus will bite my hand off.'

'Alex. You did not kill Nikki. Oceanus will know you speak the truth.' Dad's voice grew firmer. 'Now, repeat after me: "I did not kill Nikki. His death was an accident."'

I gulped and clenched my hand into a fist, and said, as levelly as I could: 'I did not kill Nikki. His death was an accident.'

I held my breath, my clenched fist shaking, but nothing happened.

'Okay,' said my father. 'Very good. Now you just have one more thing to say. Say: "I did not kill Mark. His death was an accident."'

'Oh, Dad, you know it was my fault. Everyone has said it was. He died because of me.'

'I know what they say, Alex,' said my father firmly. 'All the same it was still an accident. Now, repeat after me: "I did not kill Mark. His death was an accident."'

I drew a deep breath, and said: 'I did not kill Mark. His death was an accident.'

'Good,' said Dad. 'Now you can take your hand out of the mouth.'

I snatched my hand out of the *Bocca della Verità*, the Mouth of Truth. I ran into my father's arms, sobbing in relief because I couldn't hold my tears back any longer. It had been a horrible ordeal.

'Now, do you understand the importance of what you have just done?' my father asked me. 'People have been using the *Bocca della Verità* as a lie detector for two thousand years. You have just said that you didn't kill Nikki and Mark, and old Oceanus knew it was true. Do you now understand you were not to blame for what happened to Nikki and Mark?'

'Yes, Dad,' I said, my voice strong for the first time in months. 'I now know there was nothing I could have done at the time to save them. I'm sorry I have caused all this trouble with my being ill and in hospital. I'm sorry I have worried you so much.'

'That doesn't matter, Alex,' said my father, leading me out of the portico into the glow of the sunlit street at dawn. 'You have been very ill, and that couldn't be helped. You have psychological problems, and that we're just going to have to work together to overcome. I will always be there for you. What I don't want to hear anymore is that you're responsible for Nikki's and Mark's deaths. I think we have got over that phase, don't you?'

'Yes, Dad,' I replied. 'I think I'm going to get better now.'

'Good,' said my father. 'Now let us go and find breakfast somewhere. I think you grew up this morning.'

'Yes, I think so,' I replied.

'Then we'll have an adult's breakfast somewhere of coffee and a croissant. This morning you'll have your first black coffee with plenty of sugar. Your childhood is coming to an end, Alex. It's time to grow up.'

'Yes, Dad,' I replied.

Over the next few days I got to see the Pantheon of Rome, with its vast domed roof, the colourful Piazza Navona with its magnificent central fountain, Trajan's Column, and even the spectacular Trevi Fountain, into which I threw a handful of Lira and made a secret wish to return to Rome some day with my father.

My father got into so much trouble upon our return from Rome on Wednesday, 15 June, that I genuinely feared he was going to be arrested and prosecuted.

On our return to Cardiff we had gone directly to my grandmother's house, and she was all flustered and anxious. She told my father, quite distressed, that she'd received a telephone call from Dr Jones on Monday afternoon to ask why I had not been returned to Pen-y-Fal at noon.

'Well,' said my grandmother, 'I didn't know what to say, so I thought it best to stick to the truth. I told Dr Jones you weren't here and that you'd gone to Italy. He was furious, and yesterday, Tuesday afternoon, the police came knocking on my door, and they actually searched the house looking for Alex. I told them you weren't here, but that you'd be back today.'

My father was full of confidence and not at all phased by this tale. He told my poor old grandmother not to worry.

'I took Alex to Rome,' he said, 'and I cured him of his problems. He's better now, and there's no need to worry.'

'Really?' asked my grandmother.

She peered into my face, looking me straight in the eye, as if mental instability and illness could be seen. I avoided her gaze.

'Yes,' affirmed my father. 'Now I'll telephone Dr Jones, and tell him Alex is cured and I'll take him back to Pen-y-Fal on Thursday or Friday.'

My father telephoned Dr Jones a few minutes later, but the conversation did not go well. Dr Jones was furious, furious I had not been returned by noon on Monday, furious my father had lied to him, furious I'd been taken out of the country, furious that his treatment conducted over many months had been undermined by my father.

'I do not believe in hocus-pocus practiced in Rome or anywhere else,' Dr Jones remarked. 'We're not living in the Middle Ages, you know.' And with that he slammed the phone down on my father.

My father was not put off by Dr Jones. He instinctively knew he had done the right thing to break my anguish, my terrible fear of Nikki and Mark. Whether to old carving of Oceanus was an ancient lie detector or not, the point was my father had made me face the truth about the deaths of Nikki and Mark. Played a role, yes. But blame could not be attributed to a child, and that was his strategy. He had taken me to Rome – used ancient Rome as a backdrop – to play out a carefully stage-managed psychological game with his fourteen-year-old son to convince him he was not guilty of causing the deaths of his friends. He had used Oceanus to force me into taking the enormous leap of faith to say I had not killed Nikki and Mark.

I was very upset by all this talk of Dr Jones's anger, and thought he was angry with me. I was quite petrified when, less than an hour later, there was a knock on the front door, and when my grandmother answered it, there stood a policeman and a policewoman. Dr Jones had immediately telephoned the police after he'd spoken to my father, and my father had, rarely for him, completely misjudged the situation. When Dr Jones had said: 'I want Alex back on the ward,' he'd meant that same afternoon. When my father had said: 'I'll return Alex when I think it's best,' he'd meant Thursday or Friday. The problem was Dr Jones was the man in authority with the law on his side. I was a sectioned patient, and a minor too, unlawfully absent from hospital. The result was Dr Jones instructed the police to return me to Pen-y-Fal immediately, and that meant Wednesday afternoon, not some day of my father's choice.

I found it depressing to be a patient back on the ward after my Italian adventure, but I now had happy memories of my Roman holiday to console me, to keep my mind level and healthy. I kept Kevin a captivated audience as I told him how much fun it had been to fly to Italy, how wonderful the city of Rome was, how fantastic it was to dine out every evening at street cafes on spaghetti Bolognese, cannelloni and lasagne.

'Coo,' said Kevin. 'You're so lucky your Dad took you to Rome. The furthest I've ever been is Bournemouth.'

Yes, I can remember thinking, I am a lucky boy. My Dad has always taken me to very unusual places. But then he always demands a high price from me, I thought, thinking of my ordeal before Oceanus, the Mouth of Truth. The only problem was, which my father didn't know, was that I'd taken a terrible gamble before the Mouth of Truth. In fear of my father's anger I had intentionally told a lie; been forced to tell two lies in fact. Now I was constantly living the lie. I'd lied when I'd said I didn't kill Nikki and Mark, knowing full well their deaths were my fault. No one else's fault. *My* fault. It was now a lie I had to maintain to Dr Jones so he would consider me cured and ready for discharge.

I spent another three weeks on the ward, and had nine afternoon sessions with Mr Reese. He asked me if I was still hearing Dr Schultz. He asked me if I still believed my food was drugged. He asked me if I still believed I had killed Nikki. Asked me if I'd killed Mark.

Having endured the *Bocca della Verità* and overcome my terror that my hand would be bitten off, lying to Mr Reese came easy. No, I said, I no longer heard Dr Schultz. No, I said, I no longer believed my food was being tampered with. No, I said, I no longer believed I had killed Nikki. No, I said, I had not killed Mark. To my astonishment Mr Reese and Dr Jones believed everything I said, telling me that whilst I still had psychological problems, my time of crisis was over, and they could see I was well on the way to recovery. I now always returned to the ward joyfully, gave Judy a beaming smile, told her Dr Jones believed I was getting better, then went to seek out Kevin.

Kevin too was getting better by now. Three months of admission and treatment seemed all that was necessary to cure Kevin of his illness. Evidently there was a difference between Kevin and me. I felt a little churlish to think I'd been at Pen-y-Fal for nearly seven months, and only now was Dr Jones prepared to discharge me.

As it happened, both Kevin and I were both discharged on Wednesday, 8 July, and as we sat on our beds, coats and holdalls heaped on the floor, waiting for our fathers to come to collect us, we promised to keep in touch. Kevin came from a town called Cwmbran, a little north of Newport. I came from Cardiff, some thirty miles from there. However, we promised to write to each other, and we promised to visit for a weekend every now and again.

It was awkward for Kevin and I during those last minutes of companionship. We kept subsiding into an uneasy silence until Kevin or I kick-started the conversation again with a witty remark, or a 'Do you remember when Mr Thomas...' and we'd both collapse into fits of laughter.

Suddenly the door opened and Judy popped her head into the dormitory.

'Kevin,' she said, 'your Dad's here.'

Kevin hurriedly picked up his coat and holdall, and we hugged briefly, before he set off at a hurried pace out of Ward 3, to freedom.

'See you,' he called to me over his shoulder as Judy unlocked the ward door.

'Yes, see you,' I replied, and gave a wave.

Then it was just me, returned to sit upon my bed in the dormitory. I pondered Kevin for a long time, and wondered if we would ever really see each other again. As a matter of fact Kevin never wrote or telephoned, and I never saw him again. But then I never wrote or phoned him either. Companionship in a mental hospital is a strange but precious commodity, and I knew living on a psychiatric ward was also quite a precarious existence. A passing acquaintance could become an unstable dangerous foe in a split second. Kevin and I had trusted each other. We recognised the fact that neither was dangerous, and were more likely to hurt ourselves. I suspect the truth of the matter is that on Kevin's return home his memories of life at Pen-y-Fal Hospital were too uncomfortable, and he just didn't want to resurrect old ghosts, did not want to resurrect the friendship of someone who remembered him screaming his head off in the corner of the Day Room, or of being carted off to time-out. I possessed similar memories to Kevin, and that actually is the reason I never made an effort to contact him either.

Within half an hour of Kevin's departure, my father came to collect me.

Judy escorted me off the ward, just as Nurse Johnson brought a sobbing boy – a new patient – onto the ward. He stared at me, tears running down his face, and I can clearly remember thinking I didn't envy him his next couple of months in Ward 3.

At the bottom of the stairs Judy grabbed my arm and stopped me before we entered the public area of the foyer.

'Alex,' she said, 'you have become very dear to me, and I want to say this as kindly as I can. I don't ever want to see you back at Pen-y-Fal. Will you make a special effort to stay well? Will you be kind to yourself for any faults? Will you try for me?'

I smiled, and gave Judy a kiss on the cheek.

'Yes,' I said. 'I promise that I'll make an effort to stay well. I really like you too, but I don't ever want to come back.'

And with that Judy pushed open the swing-door to the foyer, and there stood my father.

I ran over and gave him a hug. I turned to give Judy a parting wave as my father opened the door, and I set off back to my life in the big wide world.

CHAPTER 10

# Normality

The sound of the big-band era – clarinets, saxophone, trumpets and trombones – played the introduction to the Duke Ellington song on my grandmother's record player, before Martha Tilton began to sing '*I let a song go out of my heart...*'

I will always associate that music of the 1940s with my grandmother, particularly the song '*I let a Song Go Out of My Heart*,' which had been my grandparents' special tune. It seemed to me that the song was played over and over again that summer of 1977. As the sun poured in through her French windows, still the record played on, echoing through the house as my grandmother cleaned, cooked and knitted. She was happier than I think I had ever seen her, certainly since the death of my grandfather in 1974. I think that because I was now living with her she had renewed purpose in life. It was as if the years dropped away from her, and beyond her white hair and wrinkles I suddenly saw what sort of woman she had been in the 1940s: quite a looker in her mid-thirties, and full of fun.

This I have already mentioned in my first autobiography, *Mummy Doesn't Love You*, as are the next few pages. The reality is, however, that these events took place in the summer of 1977, and not the previous winter as I had suggested in the other book. Please bear with me, and the reason will soon become apparent. I was about to be faced with peril, only this time I would shockingly do it to myself.

That summer of 1977 my father fought to stop the wheels of justice moving against my mother. Now that I was well again, Sally Martin had been at the forefront of this legal assault as she tried to persuade me to testify that my mother had tried to kill me. Indeed, only I knew my mother had tried to ruin me at Hospital X, and had then masqueraded as my Aunt Eileen to gain access to me at Pen-y-Fal to try to trick me into suiciding myself. However, after much discussion, and a considerable amount of emotional blackmail, my father persuaded me not to make any statement against my mother, assuring me that from now on I would live with my grandmother. He also managed to obtain a doctor's letter that stated his wife was mentally unstable. Sally had wanted my mother prosecuted for assault if not attempted murder, when she'd tried to kill me the previous November, but without my cooperation that would have been very difficult to prove. Social Services could do nothing more except serve my father with a Court Order that stated I was never to be left alone with my mother, ever, until I reached the age of eighteen.

My father and I had some long talks that summer of 1977, as he explained his predicament to me. 'Should I divorce your mother?' he asked me, as if it was in some way my decision, which of course it absolutely was not. My father was a man of very old fashioned morals, and in his view marriage was sacrosanct. He had loved my mother when he had married her in 1956. He was sure that beneath the surface of his mentally troubled wife of the 1970s, the same uncertain but occasionally happy woman of the 1950s still existed. There was no doubt by now that he could, with Sally Martin's support, gain sole custody of my sisters, but it was not in his heart to throw my mother out of the house, penniless and with no one to help her. Divorce was not so common in Britain in the seventies; a certain stigma still existed about it. In my father's own words, he said he had 'married *confarreatio*.' *Confarreatio* was a very ancient practice, the strictest form of marriage in the Roman world: i.e. for better or worse. This meant that whatever the circumstances, my father felt he was bound to my mother for life. He would not abandon her. Her hatred of me was, he was sure, a manifestation of *her* mental problems. She was a sick woman who needed help, even if sometimes that help was very difficult to give.

On Dr Jones's advice to my father that he should spend a lot of time with me, therapeutic interaction, my father decided to take me bird-watching with him every Sunday. Within a week of coming out of hospital, every Sunday the two of us began to go out into the countryside at dawn, or along the coast to salt marshes and estuaries.

My father was very knowledgeable about birds, recognising every sort, knowing each and every call and song long before he saw them. I must admit I was never that enthralled, but my memories of that summer are of sunny Sunday mornings with my father, and a companionship that had never really existed before, even during our trip to Rome.

We began to bond. Dad would talk for hour after hour on subjects as diverse as politics, art, ornithology and history. I had always known my father possessed a prodigious intellect, but his knowledge on all these subjects astonished me. Realising that for the first time I was more of less being treated as an equal, I found myself going to the library every week in search of books so that I could not only keep up with what he wanted to talk about, but also to contribute something to our conversations. At first my strategy was not entirely successful, for I did not know where to start and spent hours flitting from subject to subject, desperate to consume something – anything – and remember it. Then I found my forte: history, particularly ancient history.

I began to consume everything I could find on ancient Rome and the classical world, so I was at least able to contribute something to the conversation. Suddenly seeing that his son was not mentally impaired as the psychiatrists had all declared gave my father new heart, optimism that I could and would develop. He therefore encouraged me to learn as much as I could, posing questions to me about the Roman republic – its civil wars, Sulla's dictatorship, Julius Caesar, and so on – and by the next time we talked I had the answers to his questions.

In August my father took me with him to Israel, where he was working as the secret emissary for the Israelis to President Sadat of Egypt. At Israeli government expense we flew El Al first class, and were met at Ben Gurion Airport and driven by a chauffeur to a stunning top hotel in Tel Aviv, where my father had a suite all to himself. I now found myself living a jet-set lifestyle, so different to just seven months before when I had been locked away in Hospital X, my future nearly to become a life-long mentally impaired inmate and abandoned by everyone except my father. I found myself dwelling on this, and kept having to pull myself back to my new existence. I owed my father my entire life, in many more ways than just one: I owed him for rescuing me from the Attica in 1974, I owed him for rescuing me from Hospital X, I owed him for his perseverance to prove I could lead a normal life, and I owed him for the life I now had.

Menachem Begin had won the Israeli Premiership in the May elections of 1977. My father had up to now been working discreetly for the previous Premier, Yitzhak Rabin. On our first day in Israel my father took me to a substantial house north of Tel Aviv, where he met with Rabin, a man frustrated that he had been unable to secure a peace deal with the Egyptian President before the elections. I was permitted to be present at that discussion, sat out on a terrace with a glass of orange juice in hand. I heard Rabin state that if he'd managed to secure the peace deal he was sure he would have won the general election.

On the following day, a chauffeured car collected my father and me and we were driven to a large villa near Jerusalem, where I was stunned to meet Moshe Dayan, the bald man with an eye patch who was an iconic Israeli personality of the seventies. On becoming Prime Minister, Menachem Begin had made Moshe Dayan his Foreign Minister, and now my father had been summoned to tell him all about Rabin's big secret – that he'd been trying to secure a peace treaty with President Sadat and the Egyptians ever since 1975.

I'd been puzzled when my father had told me to pack my blazer and grey slacks to take with me to Israel. Now all was explained when, smartly dressed, I found myself introduced to this formidable figure of Israeli politics, and was immediately taken by Dayan's genuine smile, my hand shaken, before he sat talking to my father.

As is always the case, people lead two lives. They become someone different when at work and not at home. I now saw this facet in my father. I had seen a hint of it at his meeting with Pierre Caval in Rome, but was intrigued at the different man my father became as he talked to Dayan. Dayan asked all the questions. My father gave the answers. I had only ever seen the 'home side' of my father, a man who had often been reluctant to challenge my mother, a man who had always tried to find ways to head off confrontation. Now I sat and listened to a man who was forceful and firm. At one point Dayan asked my father if Begin could go public about the secret peace talks, and by this means force President Sadat to the negotiating table.

'No, that would be a disaster,' I remember my father replying emphatically, slapping his hand on his thigh. 'Begin can't do that! If you do, there will never be peace, because Sadat won't be able to bring his own people on side. It has to be done discreetly. We're still a long way from going public.'

My father and Dayan talked all afternoon, and as I sat out of the way listening to their diplomatic jargon my interest began to wane. I gazed about Dayan's living room at his large collection of antiquities, for Dayan was a keen amateur archaeologist.

At the end of their meeting, before we left, Dayan once more became the relaxed host. He'd noticed me looking at his collection, and he now showed me some of his more interesting artefacts. Finally, he came to a two-handled bowl of great antiquity.

'Do you know what this is?' he asked me.

'Yes, it's a first-century BC *krater*,' I said, giving the artefact its correct name. It was more luck than in-depth knowledge, for I had by chance seen a similar artefact in a book I'd recently borrowed from the library.

Dayan's single eye opened wide in surprise, and a broad smile played across his face. He looked at my father.

'Look after that boy, Peter,' he said. 'We've got a budding archaeologist in our midst.'

On our way back to the hotel, my father was full of pride and optimism. His meeting with Dayan had gone well. Yet, I think, he was even more pleased that he had at last a son he was proud of. Many years later he told me that it was during that Israeli trip that he saw that I was capable of independence; that I would, in adulthood, become a self-sufficient individual, something that not so many months before – in the winter of 1976 – he'd been told would never happen.

In September of 1977 I returned to school, for the first time in nearly a year. I was no star pupil, but about average I suppose. All in all, due to my problems, I had accumulatively missed several years of education, so it was a struggle to catch up.

Realising I was struggling in school, not only in terms of education, but also because my childhood experiences had made me a bit of a loner and I didn't mix easily with the other kids, my father decided that a different approach was needed. This was reinforced by my school report at the end of the autumn term, which stated: 'struggles to keep up' and 'reacts badly to conflict between the other pupils.'

On Christmas Day of 1977, so different to my last one when I'd been kept comatose, my father sat me down in my grandmother's sitting room, and we had a long discussion, most, it has to be said, by him.

'You are still only fourteen,' he said, 'so it cannot be expected that you know what the future holds.'

I merely nodded my head.

'No one really knows the future,' he continued with a smile, 'so you mustn't let it worry you. If you are willing to put yourself in my hands, I can set the direction. Thereafter, it will be up to you.'

'Direction?' I asked.

'Yes,' he affirmed. 'I have decades of experience in politics, diplomacy and history. Let me pass my knowledge on to you. It will give you a good grounding for whatever you decide to do in the future.'

I mulled over my father's words and realised I was being offered something unique, something I would never get even if I spent twenty years in education, which I wasn't inclined to do anyway.

'Do you agree?' he asked, mistaking my silence for doubt.

I smiled, and said: 'Thank you, Dad. Sounds like a good idea to me.'

He slapped both his hands down on his knees, a smile on his face.

'It's settled then,' he said.

And so, in the first days and weeks of 1978 my life changed once again. Whilst still attending public school, which was very expensive, my father began to augment my education with life experiences, which he felt to be important and necessary since I had up to that point missed so much of life, having spent lengthy periods detained in hospitals. To accomplish this, he began to take me with him on his foreign trips to meet important politicians of the day, and our first trip together was to take place in January.

In connection to his work as a diplomatic advisor and geopolitical expert, our first trip was to be to Moscow, deep in the Russian winter, the temperature - 20C. Here, he was to meet the Soviet Premier, Alexei Kosygin, in the Kremlin.

I now found my annoying youthful appearance to my advantage, for everyone took me for a mere ten-year-old, belying the fact that at my next birthday I would become fifteen. No one gave me a second glance as I passed effortlessly, as the son of my father, through the formidable security of the Kremlin. And then another astonishing thing happened. Kosygin, an old-style Communist of the most obdurate kind, accepted me as a child, and whilst he talked to my father about some of the most serious problems concerning the Arab-Israeli situation, I was permitted to be present, sat to one side.

I soon realised I was in a privileged position, so it was beholden on me to pay attention. Hardly anyone else in the world would have had this opportunity, and certainly no youngster. I may have had psychological problems, but I had a brain between my ears, so I listened intently to all that was said.

Indeed, at one point I heard Kosygin say: 'Of course, under no circumstances could we have permitted Czechoslovakia to break away from our bloc in 1968. It would have been the beginning of the end.'

Fifteen years later the Czechs would break away from the bloc (Soviet influence) and it spelled the beginning of the end of Communism and the Soviet empire. Thus, in my mind, Kosygin was already worried about the possible demise of the Soviet Union. He, indeed we also, couldn't have known it then, but nothing could stop the rot. It would take another fifteen years to see the fall of Communism in Eastern Europe, and with it the end of the Cold War.

We arrived back in Britain at the end of January, and with my return to school, full of chatter about my Moscow adventure, I was happy at last at the new direction my life had taken. As opposite from twelve months before as chalk and cheese. Yet in my moment of psychological contentment I was about to be thrown a googly in the cricket ball of life, and my peace of mind received a jolt. Having told my friends all about my visit to the Kremlin, I had expected interest from my schoolmates. However, the opposite happened. Whether from a lack of interest, or perhaps jealousy, my friends turned on me, and I was variously called 'child,' 'shrimp' and 'infant.' They were, of course, picking on my weakness: the fact that despite being well on my way to fifteen I still looked ten-years-old. Without exception they had all entered adolescence and their voices had broken, whilst I was still small, my voice a squeaky soprano.

Once they had left me alone, I considered the situation and resolved that in future I would say nothing more about my foreign trips with my father. Despite being somewhat upset at the reaction I had received, the event did not, apparently, do me any mental harm. I just decided to keep to myself. However, a little lurking tremor had taken place in my well-being, a seismic echo.

It was the end of March, and I was with my father in Austria. It was to be a four day trip, and on our arrival in Vienna my father hired a car and we drove into the mountains.

This was the prelude to his diplomatic meetings, but first he wanted to use this lull in the itinerary to go sight-seeing. We drove high into the Alps, still encased in winter snow on the northern slopes. It was the southern slopes, however, that had me gazing in wonder. The lower pastures were lush green and totally enveloped in a multitude of alpine flowers. It was spectacular.

On the following day my father and I were ushered through corridors and an anteroom into a large modern office, and there stood Kurt Waldheim, the Secretary General of the United Nations, a tall distinguished-looking gentleman.

It would transpire Waldheim had a secret, however, and this secret – that he had once been a Nazi – would one day cause his fall from grace. But this was to be years in the future.

In the meantime he and my father sat, with me to one side, and they discussed the secret Israeli-Egyptian peace negotiations. My father was now working for Moshe Dayan, and as I sat I heard him say that the Israelis were prepared to give the Sinai Desert back to Egypt, which they had seized in the 1967 Six Day War. I gathered from their conversation that Prime Minister Menachem Begin, who politically was of a rightist bent, was keen to get that elusive deal with President Sadat of Egypt, and whilst wanting to present a stern front for home consumption, was prepared to be most generous with the Egyptians to get a deal. I heard my father tell Waldheim that it would, of course, be a tremendous coup for Begin, and he would gain much kudos as the first Israeli leader to obtain recognition of his country from an Arab nation, something that had eluded the Israelis ever since their country was founded in 1948.

As we came away from the meeting, my father said to me, his confidant: 'I think we're going to get a deal.'

In early May my father and I flew to the Moroccan city of Rabat where we met with King Hassan. My father told me the Moroccan monarch was a secret Israeli asset. Apparently the Moroccan Royal Family had been destitute for years, so the Israelis had been giving Hassan millions of Dollars a year for a decade, so keen were they to have a friendly Arab nation. But now there was to be a quid pro quo. The Israelis wanted Hassan to use his influence with Sadat to accept their peace deal, recognise the State of Israeli, and they wanted it done quickly.

'We're almost there,' I heard King Hassan tell my father, 'but the deal will need to be brokered by the Americans to iron out the last bugs.'

My father had smiled knowingly, and said: 'President Carter is already involved.'

And so it was that on 7 June 1978, my fifteenth birthday, I found myself in Washington DC, where my Dad was to meet President Jimmy Carter in the White House.

Whilst my youth, and as my father's son, had been enough to get me into my Dad's meetings with Kosygin in the Kremlin, it was not enough to get me into the Oval Office for my Dad's meeting with Carter, and his Secretary of State, Cyrus Vance. That great democrat, Jimmy Carter, did not want his conversation with my

Dad overheard by me, whilst that obdurate Communist, Kosygin, had not minded. This struck me, I remember at the time, as somewhat ironic.

And so I sat in a chair out in the corridor for an hour, under the gaze of a rather severe-looking man with close cropped hair – a member of the President's Secret Service – who watched me intently as if I were about to steal the silverware.

Eventually the door to the Oval Office opened and my Dad emerged with President Carter, who gave me a broad and toothy smile, as was his habit and one of his distinguishing features.

'I hear it's your birthday today,' Carter said to me. 'How old are you, son? Nine? Ten?'

'He's fifteen,' said my Dad.

Carter's smile faltered. He looked at my Dad, and said: 'Oh, dear.'

He quickly regained his composure, smile restored, turned to me and handed me a pen.

'This is a White House pen, young man,' he said. 'A souvenir of your visit.'

'Thank you, sir,' I said, my voice sounding very small.

Carter shook hands with my Dad and me, and that was the end of our visit.

By the following morning we were on a flight from Washington back to London.

However, even as we flew across the Atlantic, my Dad relaxing with a whisky, me with a Coca Cola, I was deep in thought, that little seismic echo in my mind setting off small tremors. Yet again I had been taken for a child, this time by the President of the United States. If the truth be known my distress was profound. I was well on my way to the middle of my teenage years. Was I never to mature?

On my return to school I made the mistake of telling my remaining friends I had been to the White House and met the President, and it was probably a consequence of this that my last friends turned against me. Now I was taunted daily that I was infantile, whilst the reality was, in my mind, I was anything but, so this bullying became very hard to take. There was nothing I could do about it anyway, even if I'd been inclined to, which I wasn't, for everyone else towered over me. My schooldays became mental torture.

Because of my childhood experiences, and my periodic mental lapses, I knew it was only a matter of time before this constant bullying would have a detrimental effect, so I tried to keep myself aloof and never rose to the bait, and counted off the days till the end of term.

Mid-July came, and it was with relief that school finished for the summer, but by now those little seismic events in my mind were becoming ever more troublesome. Yet I kept it hidden and told nothing to my father, for I did not want to give him the slightest hint that I was having problems. He had spent the last year giving me a new life, and in my mind I felt it would be a betrayal of all he had done to tell him it had been for nothing. That I would not do, so I suffered in silence and kept up a brave face.

As a treat that August my father took me to Tunisia for a holiday. A land of camels, palm trees and desert. The heat was tremendous at over 30C, the land exotic with men in djellabas, the women in veils and headscarves. I got to see the ruins of Carthage, destroyed by the Romans over two thousand years ago, ancient mosaics in the museums, and, somehow, my Dad purloined from a hawker in the street an ancient three-inch high bronze figurine of the Emperor Augustus, who had been so venerated the Romans proclaimed him a God. In a hectic week, my father took me to see the Sahel, a land of palm trees and fertility with abundant wildlife, and out into the Sahara Desert, which to my eyes, though beautiful, was the most desolate place I had ever seen. I began to forget my problems, but this was not to last...

Far in the South, in a town near the Libyan border, we stayed in a hotel, and it was here that my seismic echo was set tremoring once again.

Having dined one evening on a meal of lamb and rice in a hot sauce, the waiter came over with an orange.

'For the little boy,' he said to my father, 'for eating his dinner.'

After the man left, my father turned to me with a smile and said: 'How quaint.'

I thought it anything but quaint, but said nothing. In my mind it felt like death in small doses.

Over the last few days of our holiday I became very quiet and withdrawn, and I noticed my father giving me sly glances out of the corner of his eye as he wondered what the problem was. It was not, however, something I felt I could discuss; indeed I did not even know where to begin to articulate my worries in words. But even in my silence my mind was working overtime as I sought a solution.

And so we returned to Britain, and I became increasingly mindful that I had a mere ten days to resolve my problem, for on 7 September I would return to school, and with it a return to the bullying and mental torture. This pressure was, I think in hindsight, causing me to mentally decline, but living the moment I did not see it that way. Without the insight to realise it had become a disorder of the mind, my seismic echo was becoming a full-blown earthquake.

Finding no solution, I realised I had apparently been sentenced to a life of appearing childlike, so I began to think out of the box, so-to-speak, and decided death would be preferable to this existence.

I left it until the last moment, but at 3:00 a.m. on 7 September, a mere six hours before I was expected to make an appearance at school, I took a massive paracetamol overdose, swallowing thirty 500 mg tablets (15 grams or about three teaspoons) which was potentially fatal. After which I went back to bed to wait for the drug to take effect.

I woke at 7:00 a.m. feeling more nauseous than I had ever felt in my life, and when my grandmother gave me a cup of tea it triggered a vomiting fit. Concerned, she immediately telephoned my father, who rushed over to see me. I was deathly pale, my pulse erratic, and still I kept retching, so he called an ambulance and I was whisked away to hospital.

In hospital an examination by a doctor, who realised I had swallowed something, elicited an admission by me of the overdose. I was immediately put on a drip of a drug to protect my liver, which the paracetamol would otherwise destroy and kill me. I was then put to bed on the children's ward, with a nurse sat next to me to keep me under close observation in case it entered my mind to pull the drip out.

Frankly, by now I felt too ill to do any such thing.

By the following morning I was feeling better, the drip was out, and Sally Martin turned up with two men, who turned out to be psychiatrists.

They talked to me for an hour and I, distraught and probably suffering trauma from what I had tried to do to myself, broke down. I told them of my nightmares about the Attica, I showed them the hideous scars I have on my buttocks and legs for the beatings I received there and, finally, I told them death was preferable to a lifetime of looking like a child. All this told in distraught sobs. I was broken. At the end of the hour, the two men nodded and left with Sally, promising to help. Sat in my bed I wondered what was going to happen. My well of woe was bottomless that day.

Later that afternoon Sally returned with my father and explained, as gently as she could, that because I had tried to kill myself, the two psychiatrists had decided to detain me. I would, the following day, be sent to Whichurch Psychiatric Hospital. As I sobbed, distraught, she smiled encouragingly and said this was to be no long-term admission. I'd likely only have to stay a month until it was established I was no longer a danger to myself.

At this point my father stepped in and told me that he now realised – had been told – my state of mind had been caused in no small part by the fact that I was not maturing. He told me he had seen a specialist in the hospital who would later that day come to take blood samples to establish whether or not my immaturity had a medical cause.

As I sat in bed, listening with tears in my eyes, I realised everyone was now trying to help me. I was not an unintelligent youngster. If all that was needed was a month in hospital, and tests to establish what was wrong with me, then perhaps something beneficial would come of my suicide attempt.

Whichurch Hospital was a fairly horrible place, with a ward for mentally disordered teenagers, the beds separated by mere curtains, and I hated it.

Within a few days the blood tests established that my pituitary gland, a tiny organ at the base of the brain, was not functioning. It is this which governs hormones. The specialist speculated to my father that my seven months of trauma and near starvation in the Attica may have cause the gland to shut down, fixing my development at that point in time when I was in the Attica as a ten-year-old. Apparently such trauma could cause this phenomenon. The cure was supplements of growth hormone and testosterone, as the pituitary gland was unlikely to ever recover. And so I now received weekly hormone injections, which would continue for the next five years. The prognosis was that with treatment I would develop and enter adolescence, but I'd never be a giant. There had been too much damage, and the condition, similar to Simmonds' Disease, though with a different cause, would always cause me to be of youthful appearance.

Whilst I was in Whichurch, the Israelis and Egyptians, under the encouragement of President Carter, agreed to a peace deal at Camp David.

Sat watching this world event on television in the ward on 18 September 1978, I saw President Sadat of Egypt and Menachem Begin of Israel sign their peace accord at the White House, with President Carter presiding.

Turning to a nurse, who was also watching this on the television, I said: 'I've been to the White House, and met President Carter.'

'Now, dear,' she said, 'telling lies means it will take you longer to get better.'

I subsided into silence, and sat quietly fuming.

If you knew what I knew, I thought, you'd not think me deranged, and I'd get out of this place all the quicker.

Towards the end of September I was visited by my Dad, who told me he'd had no idea how bad things had been for me at school; this I'd confided to the psychiatrist as the primary cause of my suicide attempt. With a smile, my father said he'd not allow the bullying to start again, and he'd organised a new school for me once I was discharged. A place where no one knew me, or knew my past.

My life, it seemed, was improving in all directions, so perhaps, in the end, some good had come out of my attempt to kill myself. I quietly thanked my lucky stars that I'd not succeeded.

I was only at Whichurch five weeks, and frankly it was quite long enough. They'd sent me there because they'd thought me suicidal, but now the causes of my suicidal ideas had been removed. I was cured.

I was discharged on 14 October, and as my father drove me home – to my grandmother's house – he said: 'I recognise you've been through some terrible events in the last couple of years, but that is now in the past, and it's no good to think about it. It will only do you harm. Now it's time to look to the future.'

As I sat next to him watching the passing streets, I had to recognise there was some truth in what he said. But the past never leaves you, and it is all too easy to find yourself unwittingly thinking about it, even if you don't want to.

I smiled at my father, and said: 'Yes, Dad. I now have a future.' And there was many a meaning in the way I said it.

# Epilogue

The ceiling fan whirred, casting dancing shadows in my hotel room. I was bathed in sweat as I lay upon my bed; the heat of a Mediterranean spring, my fear at my dream.

I got up from bed and went into the bathroom to douche my face with refreshing cold water, then out onto the balcony to gaze down at the nearby harbour, all lit up at night.

This was the Italian port of Brindisi in October 2018, and sleek yachts bobbed at anchor, the reflection of coloured lights dancing upon the water.

I leant on the balcony railing and pondered my past, pondered my late father. I had finished writing this book, and yet I still had questions that troubled my mind.

Throughout the rest of my teenage years I travelled the world with my father, from London to Lahore, from Norway to Nigeria. During this time he encouraged my education and used every opportunity to boost my intellect, spending many hours teaching me to be a confident adult with a strong sense of morality. It was as if he was determined to recreate his life in me, passing on all his knowledge to give me a firm foundation for the future, a future that was now worth living.

In a way, I suppose, my father gave me an education for the future he wanted for me as an adult. Despite my mental illnesses of childhood, my father never lost faith that I had the ability to thrive as an adult, and he did everything in his power to ensure that would happen. Perhaps it was because my father was a deep thinker, or perhaps he'd had a premonition of some kind, but he always talked to me as if he knew he would not be around for long when I became an adult. In a way he was correct. When I was thirty my father died a terrible death as a result of leukaemia, and as I sat with him through his traumatic last night of life, I found myself dwelling on the night I had sat with Nikki when he died, and the consequences in my early teens which had nearly destroyed me.

There was a glow on the distant horizon. I gazed across the blue-black Mediterranean at the beginnings of a new dawn, and contemplated my life.

In our society the mother is supposed to love and nurture her children. It has been so since the beginning of time. Yet, very occasionally, something goes amiss in the mother's mind, and this, I am sure, had been the case with my mother. She had hated me with unrelenting fervour, had tried to destroy me both physically and mentally, and when that did not work she had determined to kill me. I am sure you, the reader, will say: 'Yes, but what was the reason?' In all honesty that is not easy to answer, but I did find the utterly unexpected and astonishing reason. It took me until after the death of my father when, filled with trepidation, I returned to Greece. The truth, when I discovered it, was as profoundly shocking as it was surprising, and the root lay at the end of World War Two, eighteen years before I was even born.

My rise from mentally damaged youngster to a functioning adult who went on a mission to seek the truth features in my next book, *Redemption*, and if you choose to read it you will be astonished and shocked by what happened next. It is a tale of treachery and tension, death and my ultimate redemption, and it features a certain amount of danger, as I fought all the odds in my search for contentment and happiness. Ultimately I married in a stable loving relationship, and achieved my full potential as a bestselling author and scriptwriter for television. How I achieved this outcome is a remarkable tale.

However, the truth is that I, fifty-six year old, am still living a lie. All my adult life I have held up a bold façade before me: a strong person created by my father. I project this contented and confident façade to everyone I meet. I project confidence in my work and social life, but no one is ever quite what they seem. Deep down within me I can still too easily find the frightened and traumatised child who ended up in Pen-y-Fal; the frightened child standing at dawn with his hand held in the mouth of the *Bocca della Verità* – The Mouth of Truth. It is a daily battle for me to overcome my fears, a nightly battle for me not to succumb to dreams and nightmares of the past. It is a past that had the potential to take me in any direction: either to become a mentally fragile adult who is just about able to cope with life, or a confident adult who constantly strives to achieve. I like to think I am the latter, and for that I have to thank my father, but I also know there is a large part of the former too, and that is my own private little war.

When I'd been mentally ill I'd felt like a yacht adrift upon the ocean, rudderless and without a crew. My sanity had abandoned me. Then my father had stepped in and tried to right the wrongs he had done when he ordered Dr Schultz to alter my personality. At the time, after my rescue from the Attica, my father thought he was doing the best thing for me: obliterate the terrified and traumatised child he'd rescued from Greece. However, it had been Dr Schultz's 'treatment' which sowed the seeds of my catastrophic breakdown of 1976, which had lasted for many months. Having made a partial recovery under Dr Jones's drugs and the psychotherapy of Mr Reese, my father had made the final endeavour to cure me once and for all by taking me to Rome. My trip to Rome became a defining moment in my recovery, and my father, astute and wise, had known that a respite with him in the Eternal City would benefit me more than another month sat in Pen-y-Fal. Thus my father, finally, turned out to be my salvation, restoring my mental well-being to lead as normal a life as possible, given the circumstances. I know I'll never be free of my PTSD, but I have long been cured of my psychosis, and for that I have to thank Dr Jones, Judy Harris and my father. It is down to the staff of Pen-y-Fal *and* my father that I now have a life worth living.

The sunrise on the horizon began to bathe everything in an orange glow, and far away in the port I could see a man washing down the deck of his yacht. Life and a new day was dawning. It had taken me six months to write this book. I had confronted my mental illness and PTSD, my fear, and all those things from childhood everyone would rather forget.

I suddenly became aware that a figure – a small boy – had come out onto the balcony to stand behind me, just on the periphery of my vision. I didn't turn around.

'Hello, Nikki,' I said, keeping my gaze on the sunrise. 'Another day is dawning and I have a life to live. Perhaps we will meet again tonight...'

Read the final book in the memoir trilogy

### *REDEMPTION*

After a childhood repeatedly detained in mental hospitals, Alex's father determines to save his only son, by hook or by crook and regardless of the cost. Having started adulthood confined to a residential mental unit, Alex begins a new happier life of freedom, and has adventures in places as diverse as the Sahara Desert and Communist East Germany. But then, suddenly, everyone Alex loves starts to die, one by one, and men who would threaten his freedom reappear once more. What is he going to do? And who will save him now? The answer is his Redemption...

## Also by the Author

*THE NAZARENE SECRET*
*POPOV: THE TSAR'S DETECTIVE*

Printed in Great Britain
by Amazon